MOUNTAIN BIKE PRO

MOUNTAIN BIKE ROUTE GUIDES

THE
YORKSHIRE
DALES
and
Howgill Fells

Tim Woodcock
with
John Pitchers

future
BOOKS

Dedication
For Kay, the boys and everyone at Appletreewick

Author's Acknowledgements
Thanks first to the Dales Trail Guru, John Pitchers, for putting together the initial selection of routes – which he and his friends have been exploring for many years. Without his efforts this book would not have been possible. Also to the Officers of the Yorkshire Dales National Park for their advice and consideration and to Bolton Abbey Estate for allowing cycling access through the Wharfe valley.

For back-up and technical support: High Five nutrition (Karrimor Cycling Equipment); Shimano (Madison); John Mullett of Ralph Coleman Cycles, Taunton, Somerset (01823 275822).

For clothing and carrying kit: Karrimor Cycling Equipment (MTB wear and Elite/Camelbak rucsacs); Polaris (MTB clothing); Giro (helmets).

For hardware: Timax (Ti MTB frames); Mavic (Ceramic MTB wheels – Avenue Supplies); Halson (suspension forks), Finish Line (bike care products), Park (workshop tools), all from Madison; Ritchey (pedals); Cool Tool (trail tools); USE seat posts; WTB (tyres); Avocet (Vertech Altimeter and cycle computers).

First published in 1996 by

Future Books
a division of Future Publishing Limited
Beauford Court, 30 Monmouth Street, Bath BA1 2BW

Text and photographs copyright © Tim Woodcock 1996

Route maps based upon the Ordnance Survey mapping with the permission of the Controller of Her Majesty's Stationery Office © Crown Copyright

The moral right of the author has been asserted

Edited and designed by D & N Publishing, Ramsbury, Wiltshire SN8 2HR

A CIP catalogue record for this book is available from the British Library

ISBN: 1 85981 0330

Printed and bound by Butler & Tanner, Frome and London

Reprographics by Quadcolour, Warley, West Midlands

2 4 6 8 10 9 7 5 3 1

If you would like more information on our other cycling titles please write to:
The Consumer Book Editor, Future Books at the above address.

CONTENTS

Foreword

The Yorkshire Dales National Park has endorsed the routes in this book.

The Yorkshire Dales National Park sits astride the central Pennines in an area of gritstone moorlands, dramatic limestone scenery, characteristic pastoral valleys and attractive villages. Designation of the Yorkshire Dales was seen as providing an opportunity to create oases of peace and solitude, where the hills provide challenges and inspiration.

The Yorkshire Dales National Park Committee is a Committee of the North Yorkshire County Council responsible for the administration of planning and National Park functions throughout the 683 sq mile (1769 sq km) of the designated national park area. The Committee seeks to conserve the natural beauty of the area while at the same time promoting its enjoyment by the public.

The Committee is obliged, under the Highway Act, to maintain paths and ensure they are 'capable of meeting the use that is normally made of them'. The surging popularity of mountain biking throughout the Yorkshire Dales National Park is strong evidence that much more work needs to be done to develop prescriptions for path use and maintenance which are truly sustainable.

To fulfil its proposals to conserve and enhance the natural beauty, wildlife and cultural heritage of the National Park, and simultaneously foster the economic and social well-being of local communities within the area, the National Park Committee needs to examine more critically the relationship between the recreational activities in the national park and the environment. While being proud of its record in innovative countryside management and planning, the Committee is concerned that, without the support of the mountain biking community, additional resources and in some areas, additional powers, it will be impossible to achieve what is needed.

OFF-ROAD CODE
- **Cycle only on permitted Rights of Way**
- **Give way to horse riders and walkers**
- **Do not ride in such a manner that you are a danger to others**
- **Do not race**
- **Keep erosion to a minimum and do not skid**
- **Be courteous and considerate to others**
- **Be self-sufficient and make sure your bike is safe**
- **Wear a helmet**
- **Follow a route marked on a map**
- **Follow the Country Code**

INTRODUCTION

The Ride

The Yorkshire Dales and Howgill Fells is one of the best mountain biking venues in the UK. There's no other area that can boast such a concentration of off-road routes suited to all abilities and there's no other place in England with such sublime scenery. Uniquely intimate dales, scattered with solitary barns and hemmed in by heather moor. Stark stone pavements, grit-stone crags and river-cut ravines – the scenery is ever-changing, beautiful, and makes for exhilarating biking.

The Rider

If you're a fat-tyre fanatic, aching to etch an adrenalin-induced grin on your face then the legendary terrain of the Howgill Fells is the place to head for. A dramatic miniature massif squeezed in between the Pennine Ridge and Cumbrian Mountains, with precipitous pathways set to pitch any MTBer's mind over their matter. But if you don't want to put your heart where your mouth is then, to ensure a total contrast, seek out the sylvan beauty of Swaledale, where ancient cart tracks keep the Swale company as it meanders east to Richmond. Between these two extremes are all types of terrain, just waiting to feel your tyre imprint and implant a sense of wonder at your good fortune to be enjoying such an accessible sport in stunning surroundings. An ancient Roman road driving across Dodd Fell's sombre ridge; Wharfedale's shade-dappled pathways flicking between the trees; twisting, technical singletrack barrelling down Bowderdale's dun-coloured valley; spectacular winter sunsets seen from the high-flying tracks of Brant Fell; the wind-ruffled surface of Semer Water reflecting summer sun; the Arctic bleakness of the Whernsides in winter… All of this and more are just waiting for you and your wheels to explore them!

Twenty one fantastic rides. All of them have been planned with local mountain bikers and then ridden by the author. That wealth of local trail knowledge ensures that wherever you decide to take your wheels and test your trail skills, you're going to experience the very best off-road routes the Dales have to offer.

Making mucky round Mastiles Gate (Fountains Fell).

PLANNING YOUR DAY

The Routes

The routes described in this book are half-day and one day circular tours for off-road cyclists of all abilities. Of necessity, 'day' is a very broad generalisation as the time of year, weather, ground conditions and the riders' abilities will determine actual ride time.

Times

The time for each route assumes that the riders are attempting a route matched to their capabilities and there are no prolonged stops. If you are mixing two routes then you can predict ride times quite accurately; assume an average speed of 3–4mph (5–6kph) in winter and 5–6mph (8–10kph) in summer with a penalty of 1–2mph (1.5–3kph) if the weather or ground conditions are bad. By habitually taking note of your estimated performance in comparison with your actual ride time, you will soon get a good idea of how long your real 'day ride' can be.

Distance and Height-gain

Rides of 20 miles (32km) or less can usually be slotted into a day with ease, but rides of 30 miles (48km) and over need more careful scheduling. Although the length of each ride is an important factor, don't be a slave to mileage. For the mountain biker, height-gain is probably the most important, single determinant in the effort expended during a ride. As a rule of thumb, rides making more than an average climb-rate of 1000ft/10 miles (300m/16km) will be strenuous – you need to be fit to really enjoy them! A day with more than 3500ft (1000m) of height-gain is going to be tough, especially in winter when daylight hours are few.

Grades

Each route has been given a grading according to its combined technical and physical demands:

Fun: Low/moderate technical demands; not strenuous; ideal beginner's route or winter ride when the weather's bad.
Sport: Moderate technical demands; some hard cycling may be involved; ideal for those with some off-road experience or a 'quicky' for the fit.
Expert: Difficult/severe technical sections; strenuous riding; for the fit and experienced rider.

These grades are subjective and are relevant only to the routes in this book.

Maps

This guide book comes complete with OS maps and detailed instructions. Consequently you have no need for additional maps to enjoy the routes. If you want to explore the Dales further, the relevant Ordnance Survey 1:25 000 Outdoor Leisure maps are *No 2 Yorkshire Dales West; No 30 Yorkshire Dales Northern & Central;* and *No 19 The Howgill Fells.* The 1in *Touring Map & Guide No 6 Yorkshire Dales* gives a useful overview to the whole area. OS Outdoor Leisure 1:25 000 scale maps covering most of the routes are available laminated; this makes them less of a handful in windy weather. To protect this book on the trail, carry it in an A5 size clear plastic, zipped document case and use a book-mark to tag the route you're on. Always carry a map folded to show the terrain you are crossing.

BEFORE YOU GO

Fitness
Being fit is not just a question of muscle power. It's as much about recovery rate, and in the Yorkshire Dales some of the climbs are big and tiring. Legs that are quick to revive are not just an asset but, on longer routes, a necessity. Being in shape to take a mountain bike off-road in a landscape as rugged as this is takes time to develop. That's because fitness gains are made during the periods of rest between spells of activity. No rest and no gain. This also means that you can't significantly

increase your fitness levels in an uninterrupted session of trail-blazing. So if you're treating yourself to an off-road spree, slot in a couple of days furlough to allow that extra fitness to build.

Companions

A day riding rough stuff will be an enriched experience if you're in good company. A well-integrated team is much better able to overcome adversities with ease; even a simple thing like bad weather. Not always so simple! But trail companions are notoriously tricky to choose and in the ups and downs betwixt the beginning and end of the day there will be stresses and strains. Off-roading is not all fun. On precipitous trails it's both difficult and demanding; add fatigue, perhaps a mis-read map and a ferocious wind and you've got a pretty good recipe for a falling out. Always distressing, discord can soon develop into dispute and that could be dangerous, in the wrong place at the wrong time. Choose companions carefully. It goes without saying that you should all get on but don't forget fitness. One mis-match – couch potato or fitness freak – in an otherwise well-balanced band of bikers will often lead to persistent friction and cast a shadow over the whole party.

Summer-time trail blazing above Scar House Reservoir (The Whernsides).

Kitting Out

HARDWARE

The Wheels

I could wax lyrical about the benefits of lightweight titanium frames, tell you that suspension is a must and how SPDs are essential for smooth power transfer. Then tell you how to sell your mother and mortgage the house to finance the purchasing of that 'must have everything' trick bit and frameset. But I won't. To begin with, bike choice is a personal thing, fads and fashions change on a whim and, providing it's sound, any clunker of an MTB will do. Having said that, there are some pointers as to what makes a bike well suited to the task and what does not.

Use a good quality, reasonably light, proper MTB – 21 or more indexed gears – with alloy wheels, low gearing and a comfortable saddle. You're looking for a bike built for comfort, not speed. One with a relatively upright position, so look for a medium length, high-rise stem, wide handlebars and it's worth fitting bar-ends as they allow the rider to adopt a number of different riding positions. We're talking several hundred pounds here but if you're serious about mountain biking it's worth it. Take a look at the mountain biking press for what's what and then ask at a good mountain bike shop and buy the best that you can afford. You could also consider hiring one; there are plenty of hire outlets in the Dales. Hiring is also a good way of 'balancing out' the hardware within your group. This is especially important if, for example, one of you has a clunker and the rest are riding lightweight titanium trickery decked out with suspension. A day-long 'mega' route will amplify the difference in ride quality; perhaps putting a downer on the whole outing. You should also have your bike thoroughly serviced and checked out before setting off. A wheel buckle might well bring an early end to your day but a collapse could spell disaster, so have your wheels checked and trued regularly.

Dales trails can be pretty bumpy so there are some bike accessories that will make your off-road excursions more enjoyable: some branded, good quality treads, with around a 2in (5cm) carcass of new rubber for cushioning and grip – consult a good MTB bike shop for what's the latest trend in tyres and avoid any cheap 'imitations' as they're usually made with low-grade compound and won't grip so well; on this terrain there's also a case for some sort of cushioning, to negate the effects of riding cobbly cart track – proper suspension is ideal but one of the many forms of 'flex-stem' coupled with a suspension seat-post works well.

Tools and Spares

Quality doesn't come cheap but good tools are invaluable when you're in a fix, so be prepared to pay for them. Most multi-tools will save weight on a tool-roll of separate bits but don't forget to check that your clever widget does all the whatsits on your bike.

Once you've got all your tools and spares together, pack them tight and keep them handy – ready for the inevitable trail-side emergency.

SOFTWARE

We're all aware of the weather's profound effect on our well-being – in the wet it's doom and gloom but once the sun pops out, life's a party. It's all down to environment quality and it is clothing that determines the quality of our immediate environment. Except clothing choice is not decided on a whim of Nature. Kit yourself out with inappropriate gear that's been moth-balled in the wardrobe for the past five years and you're dressing up for a dose of doom and gloom. Uncomfortable. Take some time in selecting good-quality kit and you'll be pleased to face whatever the weather throws at you.

Even in summer, controlling warmth is the vital element, versatility the name of the game. Up on Buckden Pike it's a lot colder than down in Wharfedale. All things being equal. You can be shivering in the icy blast of a savage hailstorm while bikers down in the dale are still enjoying a summer's idyll.

Dress Sense

Kitting out a mountain biker has proved to be the outdoor clothes designers' biggest challenge yet. It's a strenuous sport, generates loads of heat at peak activity, then the loonies stand about mending punctures on a hillside with a wind-chill factor of −10°C and their body temperature plummets fast. But designers are rising to the challenge and there's a stack of really good, MTB-specific gear to choose from.

The multi-layer principle is bandied about as the way to go – and it works – but there's always someone who has to swim against the tide and now there are one or two manufacturers producing single-layer, pile-lined kit. This is really late winter wear but can prove ideal for weight-saving freaks and experienced bikers out for a foul weather foray. So right from the start we're faced with a bewildering choice of kit, complicated by contrasting design convictions and all so technical that you need a science degree to discern what's what.

The best approach is to decide what you want the clothing to do. Ideally it should be light, have low bulk, be quick drying, resist the rampant sock syndrome, be easy to care for, fit well, feel comfortable and perform well. Whether it's to wick, provide warmth, wind proofing or water resistance (unless you're a fair-weather cyclist, you'll need clothing to perform all of these functions). Above all, it has to let your body lose moisture and 'breathe'. Under-layer clothing that soaks up water, sags like a wet flannel and dims the lights when the tumble dryer's turned on, is useless. Likewise, a top-layer that's built like a tent, flies like a kite and gives you your very own greenhouse effect is best left at home and used as a bin-liner. MTB magazines regularly review cycling kit, back-issues are easily obtainable and their advice should at least put you on the right track.

Padded biking shorts are a must. There's no other item of clothing that will do so much for so little. Cut and style vary enormously and price does not necessarily reflect comfort and quality, but generally the more panels they have the better. A seamless pad is less likely to chafe and for summer biking loose fit, touring shorts will keep you cooler. Female MTBers will find women's shorts far more comfortable than the equivalent man's version. Some folk are quite happy to bike without gloves but I invariably wipe out and grit my palms when I forget to put a pair on. Apart from protection for the accident prone, padded mitts or gloves promote hands-on comfort levels, cushioning trail shock that may bruise you to your bones. On your feet there's nothing to beat a good pair of MTB boots. That's boots, not shoes. If you have SPDs check that your shoes have a deep, aggressive tread and that the cleats don't stand proud of the sole (pirouetting on a boulder on protruding cleats with a bike on your back isn't as funny as it looks!). Some SPDs also suffer from clogging when it gets really gloopy. And it can get seriously gloopy on some of the routes! There are many

Nerve-racking rut terrors above, idyllic dale below (Horse Head Moor).

alternatives to the ubiquitous SPD shoe such as light walking boots and even fell-running shoes with modified soles. Both grip well and give ankle support. Don't be tempted to make do with trainers unless you're good at grass skiing with a bike on your back. Even a modest grass bank can become an insurmountable obstacle if your boots sport an inadequate sole.

Last, but definitely not least, wear a helmet! I'm not going to tread lightly around this recommendation for fear of upsetting MTBers who want to express some notion of freedom by going bare-headed. One day you'll crack your head open and like as not it'll result in a needless call-out for the mountain rescue team.

If you're riding in cold, wet weather then you'll need to add extra clothing, especially thermals (tights, tops and socks), full gloves, headband/snood and waterproof socks. In winter, an extra-warm fleece/windproof top, for when you're caught in the open with an emergency repair, lined mitts and lined hood will also be necessary if you're tackling the high-level routes. On the hardware side, don't forget lights – all it needs is a couple of punctures and before you know it, the evening has closed in!

Navigation Aids

Your mapping is all in this book. Just add a good-quality compass on a neck cord and a weather-proof cycle computer – both of which you must be able to use with ease – and that's the pilot part sorted.

Survival Kit

Mountain biking can be dangerous; a trivial accident above Cautley Spout or a major fall on Fountains Fell can quickly bring you down to a survival situation. A matter of life or death. Carry the right kit, make the right decisions and you can turn crisis to drama, live to tell the tale and even laugh about it. Later. A good first aid kit and the knowledge to use it are essential. A basic kit should include antiseptic wipes, plasters, cohesive tape for wounds, triangular bandage, salt tablets for cramp and first aid instructions (first aid information, covering some of the common MTB emergencies, is given on pages 24–28). You might very well be an accomplished first-aider. Whoever comes to your aid might not and they, not to mention you, will appreciate a set of instructions ready to hand. Survival gear – mini-torch, survival bag and whistle – can all be packed with the first-aid kit. Pack it in a heavy-duty, zip-tie polythene bag.

In the Bag

Fell walkers are a common sight on the trail – popular walking and biking routes regularly coincide – and many of them will be strolling along with pint-sized day-packs to take their kit. Take a leaf out of their book. Travel light and leave it on your back, either in a bum-bag or, on more adventurous winter outings, in a small rucksack – about 20l capacity.

 **KIT**

TOOL KIT
Pump
Tyre levers
Full set of Allen keys
Small, adjustable wrench
Screwdriver (cross-head
    and flat)

Chain-splitter
Spoke key
Penknife

BIKE SPARES
Inner tube
Puncture repair kit
Brake blocks
Rear light/batteries
Cable ties

TRAIL KIT
Compass
Computer
First-aid kit
Survival kit
    (whistle, bag, torch)
Emergency food
    (cereal bars, etc.)
Seat pack and/or Bar/bum
    bag (to keep emergency
    kit separated)

ON THE RIDE

Fell Riding

Ride safe. Ride light. Being the new boys on the block, mountain bikers have run the gauntlet of being alienated by other countryside users since the word go but the sport of mountain biking is flourishing. Road improvements have dramatically shrunk the distance separating metropolis from isolated moor and mountain, so our wilderness areas have witnessed a motorised invasion of leisure seekers. For a time hikers (and to a lesser extent, hackers) had it pretty much to themselves but today many people have found that cycling intensifies their enjoyment of the countryside. Ramblers see us as rivals, ill-informed environmentalists call us erosionists and farmers fear speeding bikes will frighten stock and uncaring cyclists will flatten crops.

The fact that it's a re-run of early rambler versus landowner conflicts makes no difference. Neither does the fact that the hoary chestnuts of 'tyres tear up trails' and 'bikers are the beasts of the bridleways' are perceived, not proven, concerns of some of our countryside companions. But we're here to stay; entrenched attitudes are already changing and this will come about more quickly if we ride responsibly.

Rights of Way

Although we have taken every care to try and ensure that the routes described in this book will keep your cycling within the law, at the very least the status of some sections will change. Details of path changes are published in an annual leaflet *Path Changes* available from the Yorkshire Dales National Park. Write to them, enclosing an sae to the address on page 96. Plus, of course, you may get lost, so it is as well to be sure of your rights of way.

Off-road cycling is permitted on bridleways, roads used as public paths (RUPPs), by-ways open to all traffic (BOATs), unclassified county roads (greenways) and designated cycle paths. Some sections of some routes are open to us with the landowner's consent, and this permissive access may be revoked at any time. Cycling is not permitted on footpaths, open land or on pavements. Do not rely on signposts as reliable indicators of a route's status – local authorities do not always make correct use of bridleway (blue) and footpath (yellow) waymarkers. If in doubt, dismount. And remember, all land is owned by someone – even the remote moorland areas above the Dales – and you must take care not to trespass. If a landowner asks that you leave it is in your best interests, no matter what the right and wrong of the situation may be, to acquiesce.

Of course, you may be bowling along a bridleway when up pops a barbed wire fence and the way is barred. It's a tricky situation because your rights are wrapped in a woolly bit of rhetoric which says that you can remove the obstacle sufficiently to get past if it is reasonably possible or make a short detour to get round it. The landowner can demand recompense if you cause any damage so clambering over it – often the instinctive reaction – is not a clever thing to do. This doesn't happen often but Rights of Way across farmland do get blocked, ploughed up, are over-planted or are stocked with dangerous animals. Farmers are supposed to provide signed, alternative routes but if you're in any doubt don't traipse across regardless. Check with the owner and if you're still forced off the Right of Way, report it to the local authority – normally the Yorkshire Dales National Park – who will take up the matter on your behalf.

Codes of Conduct

You will not be the first to ride these routes, so you will be treading in the tyre tracks of others. If they have careered along, forged furrows across fields, stampeded livestock, left gates gaping and created a trail of havoc and mayhem then you're not going to get a warm reception from the countryside community. Nor is anybody else who follows along unless you follow the Country and Off-road Codes (*see* page 5).

They're not really a set of rules so much as guidances that any responsible, thoughtful member of the mountain biking community would adopt without a second's thought.

Ride Safety

Three's company, not two, and four's fine outdoors in the wilds. In the event of one getting badly injured someone can go for help and someone can stay with the casualty. But ideally two should go for help, not one, which is why four is better. Mountain bikers in a bunch of more than four can be an intimidating party on a narrow path.

Abilities, strength and stamina in any group will vary. Keep within the capacity of everyone, watch your pace and make sure everyone keeps within sight and sound of each other. But don't bunch up, especially on downhills, or there'll be some rear-end wipe-outs. And they can be really nasty! It's always a good idea to wait for stragglers at the top of climbs, at the bottom of tricky descents and at gates. It's in the nature of a strung-out group to separate even further at such points so make sure that the young, eager pup out in front is aware of it.

One of the first signs of fatigue is when your normally ebullient companion rides quiet and persistently lags behind. Don't push it. Rest, drink, eat and keep warm – exposure may be just around the corner. Prevention is better than cure. Eat heartily a few hours before you set out and eat lots of carbohydrates. If you expect to be riding for more than a couple of hours then make full use of the various sports recovery drinks and carbo-loading preparations now available – after all you're

Halton Gill's a well-placed watering hole for hot bikers (Horse Head Moor).

A touch of turf softens the final descent to Foxup (Pen-y-Ghent).

just as deserving of their benefits as the athletes who advertise the stuff. Try not to ride for more than hour without having some food – not as easy as it sounds – and drink regularly and drink plenty, before you get thirsty. Don't be over-confident when assessing how much trail should pass under your tyres during the day. Take into account the amount of height to be climbed – it's more important than mileage! The times given with each route are a guide and do not allow for stops. Even the terminally fit will find that thirty-odd miles or about 4000ft (1220m) of height-gain is about as much as they can do in one day.

Weather

Out in the wild, weather will make or break a ride. Outside of mid-summer you can be subjected to sun, sleet, rain, wind, warmth, cold and calm all in the space of a day out in the Dales. Maybe our highlands are minor mounds on the world map, but it can be as bleak as Arctic tundra up on the Pennines when winter gets a grip. Howgill is derived from High-gill but might better be called Howl-gill when a storm's brewing!

It's easy to be lulled into a false sense of security, set out ill-informed and unprepared and end up the subject of a fell rescue operation. Get the most recent weather forecast and make a habit of catching the latest TV weather forecasts. They give a useful overview of what's coming.

Three factors that strangers to the high moors often fail to take into account are altitude, wind and winter. As you climb, temperature falls. Roughly speaking, temperature falls one centigrade degree for every 100m gain in height (3°C per 1000ft) on a clear day, half that fall on a cloudy one. Wind-chill increases with wind strength. In a gentle to moderate breeze (Force 3, about 10mph) wind-chill is about –5°C, about –10°C in a fresh, gusty breeze (Force 5, about 20mph) and –15°C in a really strong wind (Force 7, about 30mph).

It would be foolish to venture out onto the hill-tops if gale-force winds are forecast knowing that they'll be more ferocious on the higher fells. Take a furlough and live to bike another day. And be prepared to take an unplanned detour if the weather deteriorates badly whilst you're out.

Losing Your Way

Navigation can be tricky. Keeping on course depends on you, and preferably your companions as well, knowing your position at *all* times. Danger zones are forests and open moor, and times of poor visibility are also perilous. Take care to read the terrain correctly in these situations and make no assumptions about this or that trail being a 'main' route. One way of coping with poor visibility is to follow a compass bearing to the most distant visible marker, cycle to it, take another bearing on the next marker, cycle and so on. Most of the routes described in this book take you along obvious tracks so you are more likely to feel lost than really be lost.

But, despite our best endeavours to keep you on track, there's always a chance you might wander from the route. Nobody intends to get lost and it comes as a shock. Don't panic. Stop. Re-group. Make sure everybody is with you, then keep together and only then try to work out where you went wrong. Not too far back you'll have been sure of your position. Find it on the map.

Naturally, you'll have been using your cycle computer to keep a log of point-to-point distances and it's a simple matter of reading the distance off and calculating direction, that will give you an approximate position. Forgotten to zero the trip distance at the last known point? Then estimate how long ago you were there and in which direction you have travelled during the elapsed time. Allowing for ground conditions, calculate how far you have cycled. Now check your surroundings and see if local landmarks coincide with your findings. If you're still unsure and visibility is poor then stay put until conditions improve.

In an ideal world three distinct landmarks should be recognised for you to be absolutely certain of your locality though, given two, you can still take compass bearings to position yourself. It goes without saying that correct use of the compass and trusting it, not your instincts, is vital. Many people get lost because they start navigating by guesswork instead of compass-work.

Bike Care

Before Riding A routine check-up should include brake blocks, tyres, wheels and gears. It's a good idea to keep an eye on the chain, headset, stem, cranks and seatpost. Don't forget to lube the chain.

After Riding Treat your bike kindly and it'll be a reliable friend. At the end of a day hammering and being hammered on Dales trails the last thing you want to do is bike maintenance, but at the very least you should clean (a quick spray with a hose should suffice), lube (a dose of water-displacer followed by oil on the chain) then check it over. Do this right after a ride and you'll remember all those little mechanicals that have been niggling you during the ride. Also, wet mud washes off easily; dried mud is a lot harder to shift.

Trail-side Fixers

Broken gear cables	You'll be left with a granny ring (front) or small sprocket (rear). Use the high/low adjusters to shift the mech to a middle gear
Totalled rear mech	Split the chain (or mech.) and remove the mech entirely. Put the chain round the middle chainring and a middle sprocket. Rejoin it, discarding sufficient links to take up slack, and you'll have a single-speed clunker

Spectacular limestone pavement above Gordale Scar near Malham (overleaf).

Split tyre	Usually caused by a rubbing brake block. Stop at once. Deflate and remove tyre bead from the rim on the damaged side. Place a bank note behind the split on the inside of the tyre with a margin folded over the bead of the tyre so it'll be wedged against the rim when the tube's re-inflated. Pump up and ride carefully
Taccoed wheel	Remove the tyre then use brute force to push the offending bows back in line. Rest two apexes on opposite sides of the rim on two logs or rocks, the bow curving away from the contact point. Grab opposite sides of the rim and shove down. Only one log or rock handy? Then wedge a bowed-out section of the wheel against it – or a tree – at an angle, rest the opposite sector on your knees or body and shove. Hard! No handy tree or boulder? Then whack the apex of a bow on the ground. Re-fit the wheel, adjust with a spoke key, re-fit the tyre and ride very carefully. If you still have to release the brake in order to ride then it's probably better to leg it
Loose headset	Use a toe strap or zip-tie tightened on the race to take out any play – turn it clockwise – then repeat the procedure on the lock-nut.

Accident Procedure

It's vital that at least one of the party is a qualified first-aider. Ideally, all of you should know the fundamentals of first aid. The British Red Cross, St John Ambulance and St Andrew's Ambulance Societies all run courses so, if you haven't done already, book into one. One day, somebody will thank you for it.

It cannot be over-emphasised that carrying a proper first-aid kit with instructions and being a competent first aider is an essential part of accident procedure. But first-aid instructions don't always cover the common illness and injuries associated with wild country mountain biking. These are given below:

Hypothermia

(exposure – the most common cause for rescue calls)

SYMPTOMS:

Complaints of fatigue; cold, visual abnormalities; lethargy, lack of interest; cold, clammy skin, pale in colour; slurred speech; cramps; clumsiness; odd behaviour; out-of-character actions; collapse and coma. Assume exposure if two or more of these symptoms are apparent and treat immediately.

ACTION:

Stop. Do not continue in the hope that you'll find shelter. **Shelter the patient.** Wrap them in extra clothing and put them in the survival bag, with someone else if possible. If you have a sleeping bag then use it as an inner layer. **Warm the patient** with bodily companionship and a warm drink if possible. Easily digested energy food can be given provided the patient is not too drowsy. **Cheer the patient up** – low morale is a contributory factor. Be positive – the rest of the group will be feeling pretty worried. **Rest the patient** for a prolonged period. If there's any doubt about the patient's ability to recover then send for help. **Look for signs of exposure** in other members of the party and signs of frostbite if conditions are severe. **Do not rub** the patient to restore circulation. **Do not give alcohol** – it may cause collapse.

In extreme cases, patients sometimes stop breathing so be prepared to give mouth-to-mouth, if the patient does lose consciousness place them in the recovery position. **Seek Medical Help.**

Frostbite

(long descents and winds in winter are common causes)

SYMPTOMS:

Prickling pain; numbness; skin may discolour blue or white; skin may feel hard.

ACTION:

Warm the affected area with additional body heat only. Extremities are the most commonly affected areas and can be placed in the armpit or crotch. The face can be smothered with dry, gloved hands. **Remove rings, watches, boots etc.** to ensure free blood flow. **Return to civilisation** and get the patient to hospital if at all possible or get help. **Do not rub** the affected area. **Do not apply heat** from an artificial source. **Do not use revitalised limb** or the affected tissue will tear.

Seek Medical Help.

Heat Exhaustion

(common during periods of sustained effort)

SYMPTOMS:

Pale, sweaty skin; complaints of dizziness, fatigue and headache; cramps; rapid but weak pulse; shallow breathing; fainting.

ACTION:

Shade the patient. Find a cool, shady spot and lie them down. **Cold drinks of water**, slightly salted and with a little sugar if possible, will soon aid recovery.

Seek Medical Help.

Heatstroke

(severe heat exhaustion)

SYMPTOMS:

Restlessness; frequent passing of

Above: Skippy singletrack down by Gunnerside Gill (Reeth Moor).

Left: A quiet patch along Wether Fells' unruly singletrack (Dodd Fell).

urine; complaints of dizziness and headache; hot, flushed, dry skin; rapid, strong pulse; fainting.

ACTION:

Cool the patient by placing them in shade and remove their clothing. **Sponge their body** with water until their body temperature drops and they appear to recover. **Seek Medical Help Immediately.**

Shock

(present in almost all cases of traumatic accidents)

SYMPTOMS:

Pale and pallid skin, especially the lips; rapid, weak pulse; rapid, shallow breathing; cold, sweaty skin; complaints of dizziness and blurred vision; restlessness; yawning, pronounced sighing; fainting.

ACTION:

Reassure the patient. External bleeding or other injuries should be treated simultaneously. **Lie the patient down**, protected from the ground and elements if it is cold, avoiding unnecessary movement. **Turn their head to one side. Raise their feet** on a pile of clothes or small rucksack. **Loosen restrictive clothing. Control Body Temperature** with loose clothing. **Do not give food or drink. Do not apply heat** from an artificial source. **Seek Medical Help Immediately.**

Dislocation

(elbow, shoulder and knee joints are most at risk)

SYMPTOMS:

Deformity of the joint, especially when compared to the joint on the opposite side of the body; swelling around the joint; lack of mobility; severe pain associated with the affected joint.

ACTION:

Support the injured limb in a comfortable position.

Use the triangular bandage for arm/shoulder dislocations when the patient can sit or stand, rolled-up clothes for the leg. **Do not try** to manipulate the joint. **Do not move** the affected joint unnecessarily. **Seek Medical Help.**

Broken Collar Bone

(perhaps the most common MTB fracture)

SYMPTOMS:

Patient supports injured arm against the body; head inclined towards the injured shoulder; lack of mobility in the injured side; swelling at the front of injured shoulder.

ACTION:

Position arm of injured side with fingers up towards the opposite shoulder, palm flat against the body, so far as the patient will allow. Place soft padding between the upper arm and body. Support the arm using the triangular bandage for an elevation sling off the good shoulder that encloses the elbow, forearm and hand. **Secure the arm** against the body with a belt or rucksack strap that encircles the body. **Do not move the injured arm** if it is too painful, support against the body *in situ*. **Seek Medical Help.**

ROUTE ABBREVIATIONS AND INSTRUCTIONS

The following abbreviations have been used:
Turn L: **Turn left**
Turn R: **Turn right**
SO: **Straight on**

The map, or maps, relevant to a section of text is indicated in a black box at the top of each page. An arrow indicates whether the map appears before or after the text.

Instructions are brief and to the point and follow a uniform format that are designed to give least hindrance on the trail.

Routes are split into small sections of usually less than 5.0m (8.7km) that fall between natural stopping points, such as gates, and major junctions where you can easily zero the 'trip' distance on your cycle computer. Simple compass bearings are given in brackets after each turning. A straightforward route instruction for one of these point-to-point sections would be:

'Go SO (SW) for 3.75m (6km) to go through gate into Cow Gill farm then …'.

Despite the improved quality of waymarking and signposting, off-road routes are not always easy to follow so additional information is attached. This may include through-junctions, major direction changes, fords, technical obstacles etc., together with their distance from the last point where you will have zeroed the trip distance. This additional information is provided as a running check on your point-to-point progress and is always placed between hyphens:

' – on bridleway track at first, forking L (S) at T-junction at 0.7m (1.15km) onto technical singletrack and following cairns from 2.3m (3.7km) – '.

Placed together the complete instruction gives you the direction to set off in, the point-to-point trip distance, running information (between hyphens) and your trip destination:

'Go SO (SW) for 3.75m (6km) – on bridleway track at first, forking L (S) at T-junction at 0.7m (1.15km) onto technical singletrack and following cairns from 2.3m (3.7km) – to go through gate into Cow Gill farm then …'.

NOTE TO THE MAP SECTION:

The maps used are based upon the Ordnance Survey 1:50 000 Landranger series which have been reduced by 20%. Therefore, one mile is equivalent to one inch and one kilometre to 1.6cm. The Landranger from which each map is taken is indicated at the start of each route.

Kilometres:

1 km	2 km

Statute miles:

1 m	2 m

HOWGILL FELLS

ROUTE A: RAVENSTONE-DALE COMMON (EXPERT)

Maps A1 & A2 (OS 91, 97 & 98)
Distance: 26 miles (42km)
Height-gain: 4250ft (1285m)
Time: 6hrs (dry), 7hrs (wet)
Navigation Skills: moderate/difficult
Ride Direction: anti-clockwise (dry), clockwise (wet)

A rough route but with rich rewards, Ravenstonedale is a radical ride and topping out at 2211ft (670m) gives it the biggest climb total in the book!

This ride's for the fittest only – once you've kicked those cranks you're committed to the full monty. In winter ride it clockwise – that way you can drop onto the road at Ravenstonedale if you run out of light. The significant features of this loop are the miles of technical singletrack through Bowderdale and the seriously steep spur of White Fell. Both need a high level of skill and strength to ride. For the adventurous few the hard-won prizes are stunning panoramas from the Howgill peaks and pitting your wits against a testing trail.

It's a good idea to take ten at Rams Gill ford, near the head of Bowderdale, before climbing Hare Shaw and watch out for the spectacular scenery over Cautley Spout (on your left). On top it's easy to head for the trig – don't; there's no right of way and the Commoners Association is highly sensitive to the erosion caused by trespassers. Last, but by no means least, the descent off White Fell is precipitous. Don't be deceived by the lack of rock 'n ruts and let it rip – the top's really slippery if it's at all damp and if you hit the twisty track off the bottom of the spur at speed you'll be in trouble. So will any walkers coming the other way!

Unlike other loops in this book ride, direction really is dictated by ground conditions – don't ride it anti-clockwise if it's wet. Navigation clockwise is pretty straightforward but points to watch for are:

Chapel Beck Ford: after crossing keep L up track then keep R on track then take grass singletrack up White Fell spur.

White Fell Head: aim for trig on The Calf then fork L onto minor singletrack about 0.25m (0.4km) short of it.

Great Force Gill Rigg Tarn: fork R onto descent just after tarn.

Weasdale: there's a gate on the bridge so slow down and remember to fork R at the T-junction 0.8m (1.3km) after that.

Ravenstonedale: leave on the road signed Adamthwaite.

Cautley Beck: after crossing footbridge keep beside boundary wall for 0.5m (0.8km) then go through gate into fields.

LOCATION	ROUTE DIRECTIONS
SEDBERGH	**1.** Start Sedbergh car park (GR659922) (Toilets here). Exit car park and turn L (E, on main street) for 2.4m (6.4km) – keeping L (E, on A684) at T-junction at 110yds (100m), keeping L (ENE, onto A683 towards Kirkby Stephen) at T-junction at 0.25m (0.4km) and forking L (ENE) at T-junction with unclassified road at 0.8m (1.3km) (Steep dip and bend at 2.1m (3.4km) – to Fawcett Bank farm. Keep SO (NNE) for 2m (3.2km) – on roughly contouring bridleway singletrack, forking R (NNE) across fields on vague singletrack at 1.1m (1.8km)
CAUTLEY HOLME BECK	and forking L (N) through gate onto moor at 1.5m (2.4km) – to ford Cautley Holme Beck just downstream of twin-pole footbridge.
NARTH-WAITE FARM	**2.** Swing R (NE then ENE) for 0.9m (1.4km) – bridleway singletrack vague at first then keeping L (ENE) at bridleway T-junction at 0.12m (0.2km) and taking hairpin turn R (SE) at Backside Beck ford – to Narthwaite farm. Turn L (N) in yard then immediately fork R (NNE) for 1.75m (2.8km) – steep and rubbly at first then along muddy, roughly contouring bridleway trail that turns to RUPP track

ADAM-THWAITE FARM

RAVEN-STONEDALE

at 1.3m (2.1km) – to Adamthwaite Farm. Keep R (NNE) for 3m (4.8km) – onto C-road (steep zigzag at 0.7m/1.15km; take it slow!), turning R (NE) at T-junction at 2.6m (4.2km) and keeping L (N) at next T-junction – to T-junction in Ravenstonedale.

3. Turn L (WNW) for 0.6m (1km) – keeping L (NW) at T-junction at 0.1m (0.15km), turning L (WSW) at T-junction with old A685, over bridge and turning L (SW) at next T-junction – to T-junction with gated bridleway (1st gate on R, 100yds/90m from main road). Turn R (WNW) for 0.15m (0.25km) – through gate onto gated bridleway, alongside wall, joining green lane for a time, keeping L (SW) through gate at 0.5m (0.8km), keeping by fence and then heading SO (SW) field – to gap in field wall. Go SO (WSW) for 0.25m (0.4km) – down rough track, swinging R (W) at 0.1m (0.15km) then through gates – to T-junction with unclassified road. Turn L (SW then WSW) for 2.3m (4.8km) – keeping L (W) at T-junction with C-road at 0.4m (0.6km), turning L (SW) at T-junction with bridleway/unclassified road in Weasdale at 1m (1.6km), keeping R (WNW) at 1.2m (1.9km), joining muddy RUPP track at 1.3m (2.1km), ignoring vague track off R at 1.5m (2.4km) and keeping L (N) onto tarmac at T-junction with bridleway at 2m (3.2km) – to T-junction with old A685 near Wath.

Map A2

WEASDALE

4. Turn L (W) for 1.1m (1.8km) – turning L (SSW) onto C-road at next T-junction, forking R (W) at T-junction at 0.3m (0.5km) and turning L (S) at T-junction with bridleway track at 0.75m (1.2km) – to gate in Bowerdale valley. Go SO (SSW) for 3.9m (6.25km) – swinging R (W) through bends at 0.15m (0.25km), forking L (S) onto technical singletrack at T-junction by wall corner at 0.75m (1.2km), watch out in dips into gullies and a step at around 3m (4.8km) – to ford a rocky Rams Gill (rest here; big climb starts now). Go SO (S) for 2.1m (3.4km) – keeping L (WSW) at T-junction at 1.1m (1.8km) by tarn, forking R (SW) onto minor singletrack at T-junction at 1.25m (2km), following rim of cove, turning R

BOWERDALE

WHITE FELL

Map A1

(WNW) at T-junction at 1.5m (2.5km) with obvious singletrack out along col then keeping L and on main singletrack – to singletrack T-junction on White Fell Head.

5. Turn L (SW) for 1.8m (2.9km) – very steep descent from about 0.1m (0.15km), crossing Chapel Beck at 1.4m (2.2km) – to go through gate by sheepfold. Go SO (WSW) for 0.7m (1.15km) – beside field wall, swinging R (NW) at Castley Farm and following drive – to X-roads with C-road. Turn L (S) for 3.5m (5.6km) – keeping L (SE, towards Sedbergh) at T-junction at 1.8m (2.9km) and turning L (E) at T-junction with A684 in Sedbergh – to start.

NORTHERN DALES

ROUTE B: SWALEDALE (EXPERT)

Maps B1 & B2 (OS 92 & 98)
Distance: 35 miles (56km)
Height-gain: 3930ft (1200m)
Time: 6hrs (dry), 7.5hrs (wet)
Navigation Skills: moderate
Ride Direction: clockwise

A roller-coaster route over the heights of Kisdon and Whitaside with some prime-time gnarly bits for kicks. Features part of the Wheelwright's Coast-to-Coast off-road cycle route.

A brilliant summer's day ride with plenty of scope to tailor it to suit shorter times. It's quite a climb up to Apedale Head but the 1000ft (300m) drop back down to the Swale is an entertaining mix-and-match batch of singletrack, road and rutted track. It's easy to over-shoot the field gate accessing the track down to Low Houses. From there to Kidson it's pootle-time with an opportunity to down a pint in Muker. Kidson marks a return to granny-cogging; height-gain is impressive as are the views down Swaledale. Suddenly it all

continued on page 36 ...

MAP A1 RAVENSTONEDALE COMMON

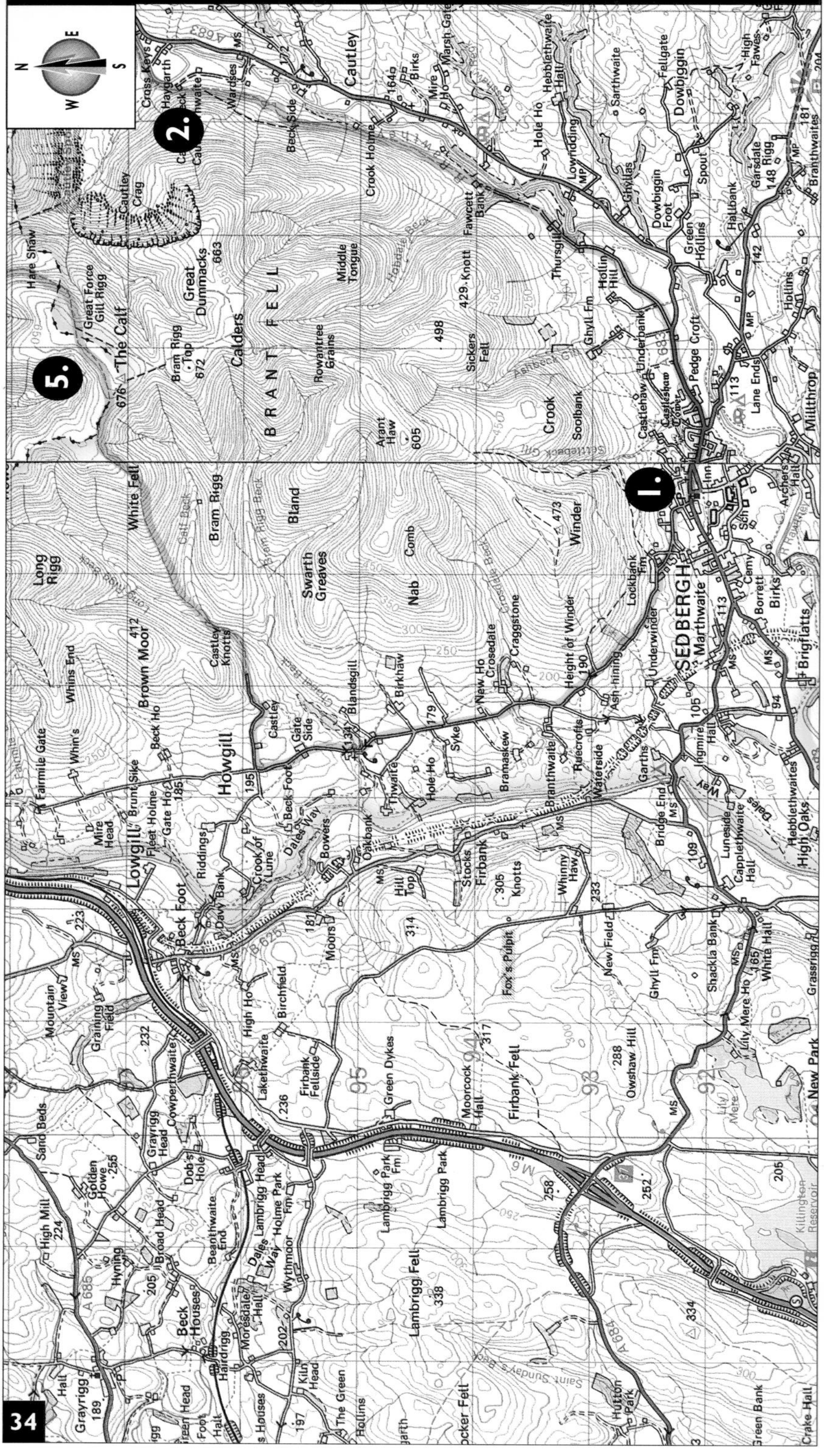

N
W E
S

Ravenstonedale
Moor

Cairn
Fell
Begin
Hill
Settlement
Bents
Smardale

Brackenber
Earthwork
Smardale Br
327
Rasett
382

Brownber
272
Friar's Bottom Fm
Ashfield
Hill Top
249
Dubbs
Newbiggin-on-Lune
Coldbeck
244
Garshill
Claylands Fm

Rigg End
257
318

Potlands

Long Gill
ebridge
Bowderdale

252
Gars

Scar Sikes
The Lane
Trahmoor
Moss
Sandwath
255
Earthwork
Earthwork
276
Kilnmire
271
Piper Hole
Row Foot
284
Lockholme
The Green
Artlegarth

Weasdale
Pinskey Bottom
Greenside
Greenside Tarn
Wath

4.

3.

Ravenstonedale

Stwarth
03

289

Hooksey

Great Swindale
02

West Fell
541
West Grain
Green Bell
605
Knoutberry
464 Knott
369
Banks
Ellergill
291

R A V E N S T O N E D A L E   C O M M O N
586
Spengill Head
Grere Fell
70
71
404
Harter Fell
522
Studfold
MS
295
73

67
68
Leathgill Bridge
69
Randygill Top
624

578
Hazelgill Knott
Kensgriff
574
374
Adamthwaite
368
Sandbed
275
Cold Keld
Springgill
Low Dovengill

W G I L L
E L L S
Yarlside
639
Wandale Hill
497
Mountain View
Murthwaite
226
Elm Pot
Fell End
Streetside
Foggy Gill
Black Moss

5.
Hare Shaw
Great Force Gill Rigg
The Calf
Cautley Crag
Ben End
Narthwaite
Handley's Br
195
MS
Bridge Cottages
Rawthey Br
Tarn
Eller Hill
White Green

2.
Frogs Keys
Haygarth
Cautley Beck
Cautley Thwaite
Wardses
MS
345
Bluecaster
Needle Ho
Uldale Ho

ram Rigg Top
972
Great Dummacks
663
Calders

N T   F E L L
Beck Side
Bluecaster Side
96
Taythes
Taythes Beck Wood
Raven Thorn

owantree Grains
Middle Tongue
Crook Holme
Cautley
96
W e s t   B a u g h   F e l l

498
Sickers
429 Knott
Fawcett
164
Birks
Mire Ho
Marsh Gate

turns Pennine-like on top – bleak, far-flung fells surround – before the trail bounces down to Keld.

A tarmac interlude sets you up for a scenic saunter down the Pennine Way. If it's a fine summer's afternoon you're in for some real soul biking from here on in. The track past Crackpot is one of the best bits of biking along the *Wheelwright's* Coast-to-Coast cycle route; once a simple cart track it makes for an exciting roller-coaster ride with tricky climbs and enough rough stuff to make top-cogging on descents a touch risky. Watch out for the gate down by Swinner Gill though! The valley's verdant, the views gorgeous – literally! If you're tempted to forgo the climb up past Heights then think again; especially on a summer's evening. There's no better spot to see Swaledale from.

GRINTON LODGE

1. Start at Grinton Lodge YHA (GR048976) and from entrance zigzag R/L (effectively SO, W) onto bridleway for 1.1m (1.75km) – turning L (SSW) onto C-road at 0.12m (0.2km) – to T-junction then fork R (SW) onto waymarked bridleway on How Hill for 1.75m (2.8km) – singletrack feint at first, passing twin cairns on Greets Hill then swing L (S) after gate at 0.75m (1.2km) – to track T-junction at Dent's Houses.

GREETS HILL

APEDALE HEAD

2. Turn R (W) for 2.3m (3.7km) on Apedale Head track – turning L (SW) at 2.2m (3.5km) and swinging R (WNW) past large cairn – to go through gate in fence. Swing R (NW) for 1.5m (2.4km) – soon to swing L (W) through tips on boggy singletrack then R (NW) onto track – to T-junction with C-road. Turn R NE) for 1m (1.6km) – over cattle grid – to gate at High Lane.

3. Turn L (WSW) through gate for 0.5m (0.8km) – across field then through RH gate onto track – to T-junction with C-road in Low Houses. Turn L (WSW) for 2.4m (3.8km) – keeping SO (W) at T-junction at 0.3m (0.5km), forking R (W) at 'dead-end' T-junction at Haverdale at 0.6m (1km) onto Dubbing Garth Lane – to B6270. Keep SO (W) for 2.5m (4km) to Muker then turn R (NNE) for 0.15m (0.25km) – into Muker and zigzagging L/R onto waymarked bridleway track – to gate at Ford.

HAVERDALE

MAP B2

4. Go through (N then W) for 0.8m (1.3km) – track zigzags at first then fork R (WNW) at 0.5m (0.8km) up walled track, keeping SO (NNW) at 0.7m (1.15km) by wall on L – to gate. Go SO (N) for 1.5m (2.4km) – keeping to wall on R to corner then turning L (W then NW) on gated grass singletrack, joining gated track at 0.5m (0.8km) near sheepfold and crossing ford at 1.4m (2.2km) – to B6270.

KELD

5. Turn R (NNE) for 1.9m (3km) – past Keld and turning R (N) onto C-road at 0.9m (1.4km) – to T-junction with bridleway track. Fork R (N) for 0.6m (0.4km) up to T-junction with Pennine Way. Turn R (S) for 1.5m (2.4km) to East Stonesdale farm. Go SO (SSE) for 0.1m (0.15km) – crossing gated farmyard, passing T-junction where Pennine Way turns R – to gated bridge above falls. Keep SO (ESE)

CRACKPOT

for 4m (6.4km) – keeping R (SE) at Crackpot fork at 0.75m (1.2km), joining C-road at Ramps Holme farm at 2.6m (4.2km) – to T-junction near Ivelet.

MAP B1

6. Turn L (N then E) for 1.1m (1.75km) to X-roads in Gunnerside then keep SO (E) on B6270 for 0.15m (0.25km) to steel gate on L. Fork L (ENE) for 0.75m (1.2km) – up drive, keeping L of house, SO onto walled singletrack bridleway leaving Heights Ho to R at 0.4m (0.6km) then singletrack keeps topside of wall before swinging L (N) at 0.7m (1.15km) up field – finally to swing R (SE) through gate. Keep SO (SE then E) for 0.5m (0.8km) to 1st wall corner then turn R (SSE) for

SMARBER

0.75m (1.2km) – between walls to Smarber, keeping L, through gate then following track (E) – to T-junction with B6270 in Low Row.

7. Turn R (WSW) for 0.9m (1.4km) – turning L (SSW) at first T-junction at 0.25m (0.4km), across bridge, L (E) at next T-junction at 0.6m (1km) – to

LOW HOUSES

Low Houses then fork L (NE) for 2.3m (3.7km) – on Low Lane track joining C-road at 1.5m (2.4km), keeping SO (E) at T-junction at 1.7m (2.7km) and over cattle grid – to T-junction with singletrack bridleway off L. Turn L (NNE) for 50yds (45m) to

MAP B1 SWALEDALE

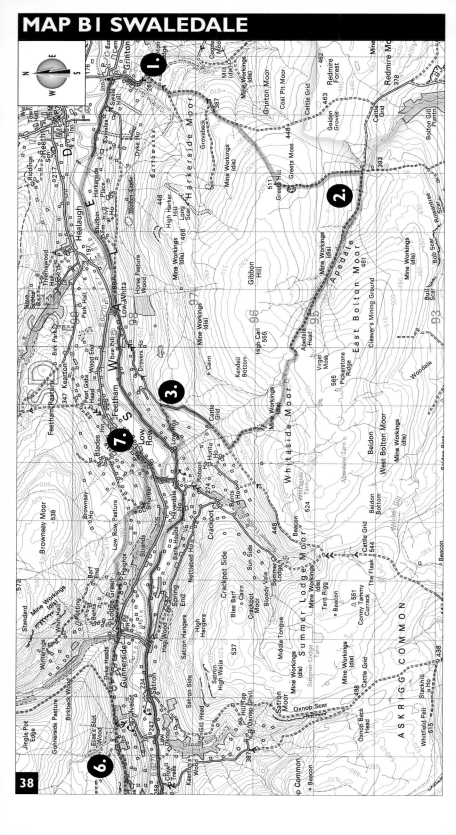

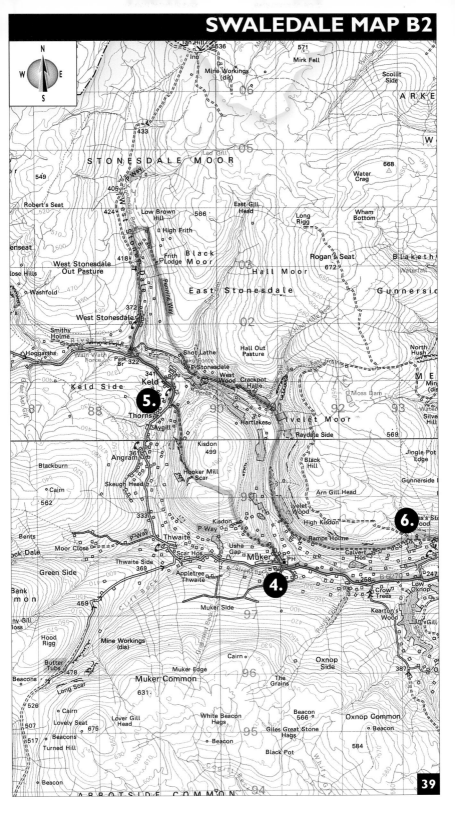

STUBBIN FARM go through gate. Swing R (NE) for 2.3m (3.7km) – on singletrack below Stubbin Farm, through gated fields and joining C-road by Swale Hall at 1.8m (2.9km) – to Grinton then turn R (S) for 0.6m (1km) – keeping SO (SSE) at T-junction at 0.4m (0.6km) – to Grinton Lodge YHA and start.

SWALE HALL

ROUTE C: REETH MOOR (SPORT)

MAP C1 (OS 92 & 98)
Distance: 25 miles (40km)
Height-gain: 3500ft (1060m)
Time: 4hrs (dry), 5hrs (wet)
Navigation skills: moderate
Ride Direction: either way

Scoot round the old mining tracks of Marrick and Reeth plus a jaunt across the lunar landscape that's the Melbeck Moors. All that adrenalin-inducing trail blazing finishes off with a heady mix of techno-track and scenic sauntering down the Dale home.

Thankfully tarmac takes you up Fremington Edge; its 1000ft (300m) vantage gives fine views over the dales down below. A thriving mining industry has left a legacy of mining tracks to ride and it is one of these that we join at the road end. Puddled and pot-holed it's fun to ride, especially the twisty dip down into Storthwaite Farm. Be sure to follow route directions carefully – tracks are numerous and it's easy to be misled in the mist. On Great Pinseat there isn't a single blade of grass; it's an eerie setting, especially when mists swirl and curl around. Acres of dead white spoil heaps where lead has left the soil bereft of life. It makes ideal riding though!

More meandering mine tracks – with the occasional dip and dive to liven things up – take you round to Blakenthwaite's craggy cleft in the heather. It's a steep drop down, round the valley head to the gill. Then things turn a touch technical, singletrack rules for a time after which it's back to track – this time with gravity on your side – all the way down to Gunnerside; nearly! You'll have to weigh up the pros and cons of the optional hoick over the Heights – the views are excellent.

REETH

1. Start in Reeth (GR038993). Take B6270 (E) 0.6m (1km) to T-junction on RH bend in Low Fremington then keep L (ESE) on lane for 20yds (18m) to turn L (NNE) for 0.75m (1.2km) – into Fremington, zigzagging L/R at 100yds (110m) – up to gate. Go SO (N) for 1.5m (2.4km) – over Fremington Edge – to Hurst Farm.

HURST FARM

2. Turn L (WSW) for 1.1m (1.75km) – on bridleway track, swinging L (W) onto singletrack at 0.8m (1.3km) R (NW) by fence – to gate on inside of corner. Go SO (WNW) through gate for 1m (1.6km) – following singletrack through tips, swinging L then R at 0.5m (0.8km) – to gate. Go SO (S) 0.15m (0.25km) to Storthwaite Hall Farm then turn R (E) for 1m (1.6km) on track to Langthwaite.

LANG-THWAITE

3. Turn L (SE) immediately over bridge then turn L (S, towards Raw) for 0.75m (1.2km) to waymarked T-junction with bridleway. Turn R (SW, NW then W)) for 1.5m (2.4km) – round spur – to T-junction with C-road at Fore Gill gate. Turn L (W then S) for 3m (4.8km) – through ford, turning R (WNW then NW) onto bridleway track at T-junction at 0.4m (0.6km), swinging L (NW) by sheepfold at 2m (3.2km) over Great Pinseat tips and following cairns from 2.25m (3.6km) then descending L (W) – to go through gate.

GREAT PINSEAT

4. Turn L (S) for 3.3m (5.3km) – through ford then down track, turning R (WNW) over Level Ho Bridge at 0.6m (1km), through tips on bridleway track and keeping SO (W) at T-junction at 1m (1.6km), keeping R (WNW) at T-junction at 1.75m (2.8km) and turning L (NW then W) at T-junction with singletrack (vague; head up valley) by fords at Blakenthwaite Mines at 3m (4.8km) – to dam.

BLAKEN-THWAITE

5. Take hairpin turn L (ESE) (care! Steep drop to stream) for 3.6m (5.8km) – on technical singletrack, forking R (SSE) at T-junction at 0.75m (1.2km), over ford and picking up track at North Hush – to T-junction with C-road at Dyke Heads.

DYKE HEADS

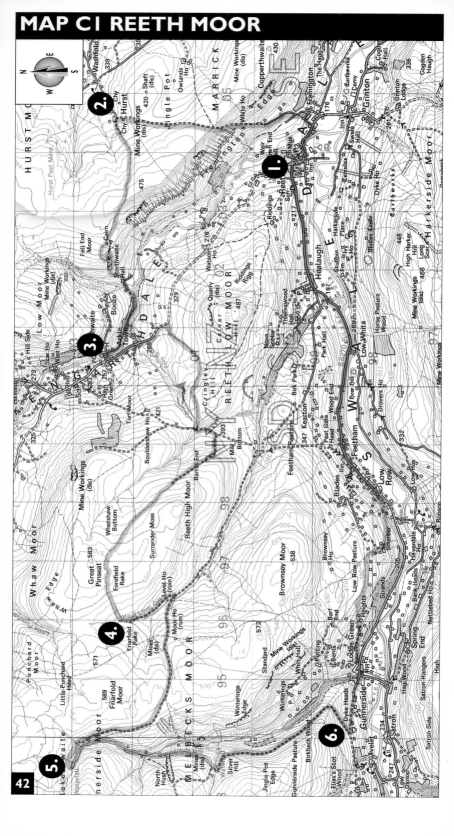

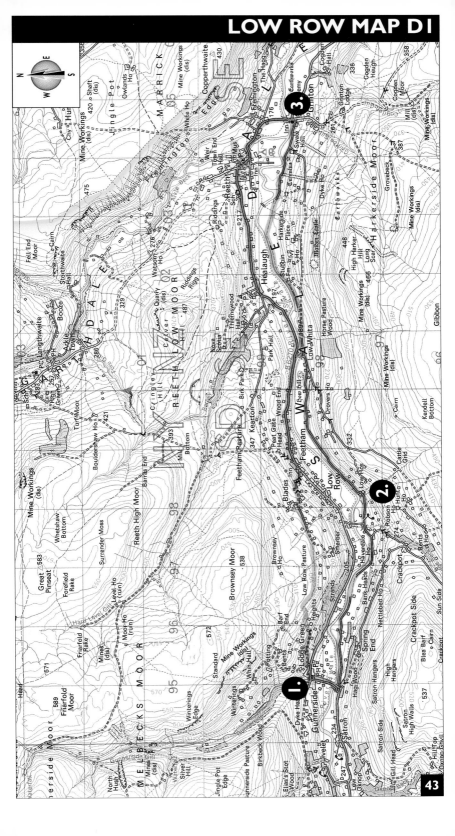

GUNNER-SIDE

6. Turn L (E) for 1.1m (1.75km) to X-roads in Gunnerside then keep SO (E) on B6270 for 0.15m (0.25km) to steel gate on L. Fork L (ENE) for 0.75m (1.2km) – up drive, keeping L of house, SO onto walled singletrack bridleway leaving Heights Ho to R at 0.4m (0.6km) then singletrack keeps topside of wall before swinging L (N) at 0.7m (1.15km) up field – to swing R (SE) through gate. Keep SO (SE then E) for 0.5m (0.8km) to 1st wall corner then turn R (SSE) for 0.75m (1.2km) – between walls to Smarber, keeping L, through gate then following track (E) – to T-junction with B6270 in Low Row. Fork L (NE) for 4m (6.4km) road ride to Reeth.

LOW ROW

ROUTE D: LOW ROW (FUN)

MAP D1 OS 98
Distance: 15 miles (24km)
Height-gain: 950ft (290m)
Time: 1.5hrs (dry), 2.5hrs (wet)
Navigation Skills: easy
Ride Direction: either way

An ideal low-level route for beginners but take care on the tarmac sections, especially in summer. In winter and in the wet be prepared for mud and puddles.

GUNNER-SIDE

1. Start Gunnerside (GR951982) and take B6270 towards Muker and Keld (W then S) for 0.5m (0.8km) – across bridge – to T-junction then turn L (E) for 20yds (20m) to T-junction with Dubbing Garth Lane track. Fork L (ENE) for 2.5m (4km) – joining C-road at 1.75m (2.8km) and going SO (E) at T-junction at 1.9m (3km) – to lane end at Low Houses.

LOW HOUSES

2. Fork L (NE) for 2.3m (3.7km) – on Low Lane track then joining C-road at 1.5m (2.4km), keeping SO (E) at T-junction at 1.7m (2.7km) and over cattle grid – to T-junction with singletrack bridleway off L. Turn L (NNE) for 50yds (45m) to

| STUBBIN FARM | go through gate. Swing R (NE) for 2.3m (3.7km) – on singletrack below Stubbin Farm, through gated fields and joining C-road by Swale Hall at 1.8m |
| GRINTON | (2.9km) – to Grinton. |

3. Turn L (N) for 4.5m (7.2km) – going SO (N) onto B6270 at 50yds (45m) and passing through Reeth and Healaugh – to T-junction with C-road in **FEETHAM** Feetham just past Punchbowl Inn. Fork R (W) for 1.5m (2.4km) – joining bridleway track at 0.8m (1.3km) and SO (W) at track junction at 1m (1.6km) – to go through gate. Zigzag L/R (W, S then W) for 0.8m (1.3km) – going downhill, pass **HEIGHTS HO** Heights Ho, joining walled track, then singletrack and keeping L (WSW) on lane at 0.7m (1.15km) and through gate – to B6270 in Gunnerside. Fork R (W) 0.12m (0.2km) to start.

WENSLEYDALE

ROUTE E: BOLTON MOOR (FUN)

MAP E1 (OS 98)
Distance: 16 miles (26km)
Height-gain: 1880ft (570m)
Time: 2.5hrs (dry), 3hrs (wet)
Navigation Skills: moderate
Ride Direction: clockwise

A double dose of scenics in this dale-to-dale hop that finishes with a couple of prime-time track runs.

A farm track that contours for the most part, giving your limbs time to warm up before a touch of tarmac torture. The climb over The Fleak. Don't ignore the views opening out behind – they're an ideal excuse to stop and give the heart-rate time to simmer down. The drop off The Fleak is fast, furious and twisty too; take care!

After all that freewheeling slipstream roar on the steep sweep

continued on page 48 ...

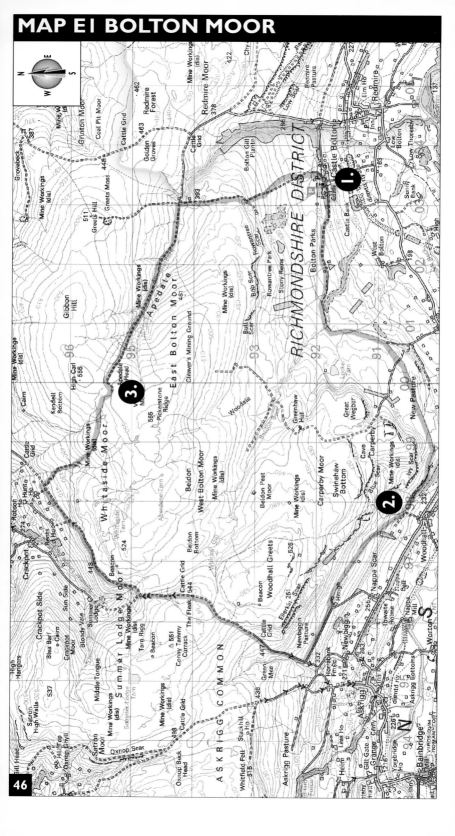

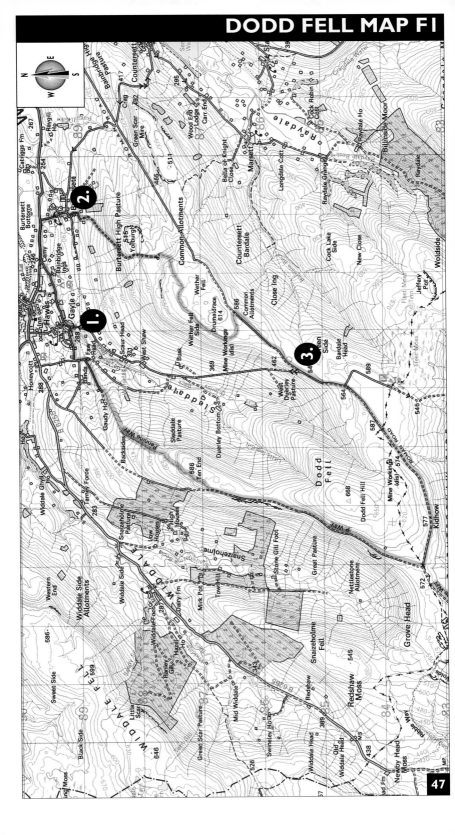

into Swaledale, the tricky track climb up to Apedale Head comes as a bit of a shock. But once you're up – watch the wheel-grabbers along the singletrack to the top – it's downhill all the way home; nearly! Apedale has a couple of unexpected ups to give the legs a work-out. Do a right at Dents, crest Black Hill and relax for some prime-time track cruising back to Bolton.

CASTLE BOLTON

1. Start Castle Bolton car park (GR033919). Turn R (W) for 1.6m (2.6km) – on gated track – to gate onto bridleway grass track. Swing L (S) for 2.5m (8km) – forking L (SW, towards Askrigg) at signed bridleway T-junction at 0.5m (0.8km), SO fields and joining track at 2m (3.2km) – to go through gate.

2. Zigzag L/R (effectively SO) (NW) and immediately join track for 2m (3.2km) – track becomes walled then keeping R (WNW) at T-junction at 1.4m (2.2km) – to T-junction with C-road. Turn R (NNE) for 3.6m (5.8km)(steep and twisty descent into Swaledale – take care!) to T-junction with signed bridleway track off R. Turn R (S, E then SE, towards Castle Bolton) for 1.4m (2.2km) – keeping SO (SSE) at T-junction at 0.5m (0.8km) then following cairns, swinging R (S then E) at 1.2m (1.9km) – to go through gate at Apedale Head.

APEDALE HEAD

3. Go SO (ESE) on track for 3.8m (6.1km) – immediately passing large cairn, swinging L/R (NE then E), turning right at track X-roads at Dent's Houses at 2.3m (3.7km) and joining walled track at 3.2m (5.1km) – to T-junction with C-road in Castle Bolton. Turn R (W) 0.1m (0.15km) to start.

ROUTE F: DODD FELL (SPORT)

MAP F1 (OS 98)

Distance: 13 miles (21km)
Height-gain: 1350ft (410m)
Time: 2hrs (dry), 2.5hrs (wet)
Navigation Skills: easy/moderate
Ride Direction: either way

Short and sweet, the meat of this loop lies in the contour-hopping climb (or descent) above Burtersett. An ideal mate for an expert figure of eight with Route G.

Basically a one up and one down, this loop begs to be ridden both ways. As written, the road ride allows a warm-up before the lung-busting climb from Burtersett. As a technical downhill, wheel-grabbing ruts are set to test both nerve and skill. Don't wander onto Wether Fell – the obvious path heads straight across then peters out amidst peat hag. The bridleway keeps by the inside of the northern wall, but beware of abrupt drop-offs and dips, that call for a 100% commit-and-crank routine. On an anti-clockwise loop watch out for stone steps about 1m (1.6km) from Cam High Road. Half the loop follows the Pennine Way so please ride with consideration for walkers.

GAYLE   **1.** Start Gayle Beck Bridge, Gayle (GR871893). Take C-road (ENE, towards A684 and Bainbridge) for 1.7m (2.7km) – turning R (E) onto A684 (busy road; take care!) at 0.75m (1.2km), turning R (SSE, towards Burtersett) at T-junction with minor C-road at 1.2m (1.9km) and forking R (SW) at T-junction at 1.6m (2.6km) in Burtersett – to T-junction with bridleway track.

2. Turn L (S) for 1.7m (2.7km) – obvious track zigzags R then L, gets steep and very rough then crests col at 1m (1.6km), turning R (SW) at T-junction with footpath on col at 1.25m (2km), keeping R (W) at T-junction with vague bridleway at 1.4m (2.2km) and keeping L (W) at singletrack T-junction at 1.6m (2.6km) – to go through gate onto

WETHER   Wether Fell. Fork R (W) for 1.4m (2.2km) –
FELL   keeping alongside wall on vague singletrack at first with sudden peat cut at 0.9m (1.4km) and dips at

1m (1.6km) – to signed bridleway/track T-junction. Turn R (SW) for 1m (1.6km) to T-junction with C-road.

3. Fork L (SSW) for 2.7m (4.3km) – keeping R (SSW) at T-junction at 0.4m (0.6km) onto gated C-road – to T-junction with Pennine Way (signpost) bridleway track just after Kidhow Gate.

KIDHOW GATE

Turn R (NNE) for 4.1m (6.6km) – forking R (NNE) at track/singletrack Pennine Way (waymarker) T-junction at 2.4m (6.4km) – to go through gate onto Gaudy House access. Turn R (ENE) for 0.8m (1.3km) – (drainage runnels!) turning L (N) at next T-junction, keeping R (N) at T-junction at 0.4m (0.6km), turning R (E, towards Gayle) at T-junction at 0.5m (0.8km) and keeping SO (ENE) at junctions that follow – to start.

GAUDY HOUSE

ROUTE G: GREEN SCAR (SPORT)

MAP G/H I (OS 98)
Distance: 14.5 miles (23km)
Height-gain: 1650ft (500m)
Time: 2.5hrs (dry), 3hrs (wet)
Navigation Skills: easy
Ride Direction: either way

A real Dales trail taster. Add it to Route F for an expert 'figure-of-eight'. See Route H for a simpler version.

The old Roman Road out of Bainbridge is a case of mind over matter – a helmet peak helps. It doesn't test the legs until the very last so just keep plugging along. The views over Semer Water strive for your attention as you tackle the techno-singletrack descent down to Countersett. Beware of the switch-backs on the road though!

From Semer the long, measured climb back up to Stake Allotments is mostly track. This makes for an exciting, non-technical, top-cog descent if you're riding the loop clockwise. Half-way down to Carpley Green Farm the rough track hangs a left and steepens. Ideal pinch-puncture territory if you're hammering! Again, watch out on the twisty tarmac at the end.

GREEN SCAR & SEMER WATER G/H 1

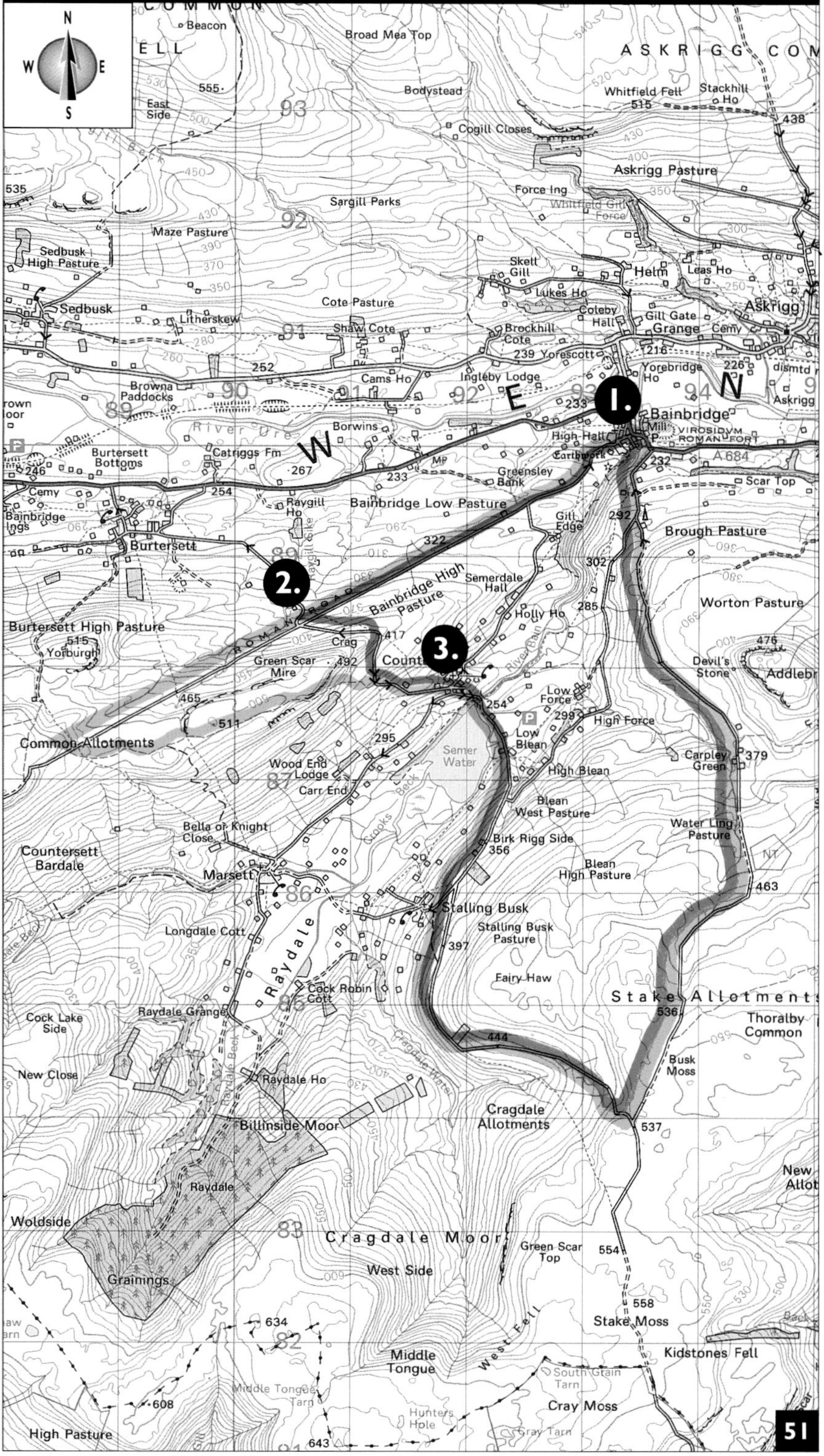

ROUTE H: SEMER WATER (FUN)

Map G/H I (OS 98)
Distance: 12 miles (19km)
Height-gain: 1300ft (400m)
Time: 2.5hrs (dry), 3hrs (wet)
Navigation Skills: easy
Ride Direction: either way

A version of Route G with the technical taken out. Take care on the tarmac descents – all sport some seriously sharp bends.

BAINBRIDGE

1. Start top side of Bainbridge green (GR934902). Leave village on minor C-road heading towards Countersett and Semer Water (S then SW) for 2.2m (3.5km) – keeping R (WSW) onto track at T-junction at 0.75m (1.2km) – to track/C-road X-roads.

2. Fun Route: turn L (ESE) onto C-road for 1.25m (2km) – over hill and watch sharp LH bend at 0.75m (1.2km) – to staggered X-roads in Countersett and pick up Sport Route at para No 3. **Sport Route**: Go SO (WSW) for 1.5m (2.4km) up track to T-junction with bridleway. Turn L (SE) for 1.4m (2.2km) – on rutty track, keeping L (E) at T-junction with waymarker at 0.2m (0.3km), swinging L/R (effectively SO) round shake hole immediately after 1st gate, through wall gap, going SO (ENE) at waymarker at 0.5m (0.8km) and waymarker at 0.6m (1km) – to go through gate. Swing R (E) for 0.6m (1km) – down twisty, rubbly singletrack and swinging R/L at gate at 0.5m (0.8km) – to C-road. Turn R (E) for 0.5m (0.8km) to staggered X-roads in Countersett.

COUNTER-SETT

3. Zigzag R/L (effectively SO) (E) for 3.5m (5.6km) – (sharp RH bend after bridge!) keeping R (SSW, towards Stalling Busk) at T-junction at 0.6m (1km) and forking L (S) onto High Lane track at 1.1m (1.8km) – to track T-junction with signpost

STALLING BUSK

BUSK MOSS on Busk Moss. Turn L (NNE) for 4.3m (7km) – on green lane, track then tarmac after Carpley Green farm (steep with sharp bends!) and keeping R (N) at T-junction at 4m (6.4km) – to T-junction with A684. Turn L (W then NW) for 0.25m (0.4km) back into Bainbridge.

LANGSTROTHDALE CHASE

ROUTE 1: LANGSTROTH-DALE AND OUGHTERSHAW (EXPERT)

MAPS 11, 12 & 13 (OS 98)
Distance: 38 miles (61km)
Height-gain: 3680ft (1115m)
Time: 7hrs (dry), 9hrs (wet)
Navigation Skills: easy
Ride Direction: clockwise

This ride meanders through the most remote regions in the Dales. Mostly track, the loop saves the best until last on the long drop to Buckden.

The longest loop route in the book, but with plenty of opt-outs. It's tarmac to Green Field Forest then track sweeps you over Birkwith Moor and down to Horton in Ribblesdale on the Pennine Way (watch out for walkers), then a little-used lane climbs steadily up to Old Ing. It's rump-rattle track to Ling Gill Bridge, then 4 × 4 boys create mega-ruts and puddles all the way up to the road out of Cam Houses.

For a while the route shares tyre tracks with Sport Route G, spins along the top of Stake Moss then amble-time abruptly ends in the shattered track that drops down to the Buckden road. A short, tarmac switch-back then it's back to track where the fun finale is a skip 'n skid, top-cog descent down to Buckden, but don't click in the big ring unless it's mid-week or late in the day. The climb up from the car park is Joe-Public's ideal, half-hour out with the dog. And a warning if it's wet; the pedestrian polished limestone is slicker than a snail trail.

MAP II LANGSTROTHDALE CHASE

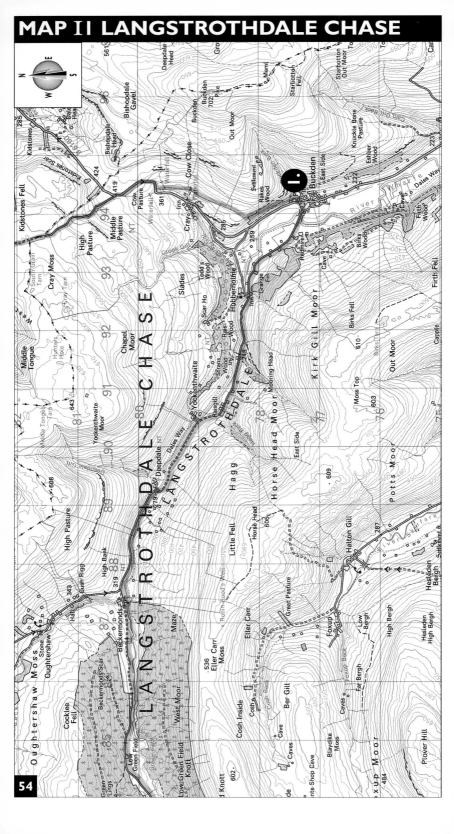

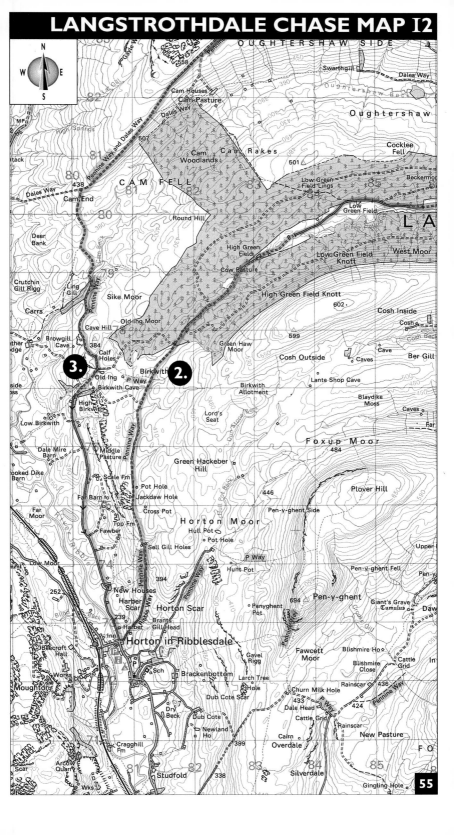

BUCKDEN

1. Start Buckden car park (GR774943). Turn L (S, out of main entrance) for 8m (12.8km) – on B6160 at first, turning R (W) at T-junction with track at 100yds (100m), turning R (WNW) onto C-road at 0.1m (0.15km), keeping L (WNW) at T-junction at Hubberholme at 1.25m (2km) and turning L (W) at T-junction at 5m (8km) – to go through gate onto track at High Green Field. Keep SO (SW) for 1.25m (2km) – forking L (SW) at T-junction at 0.7m (1.15km) – to track T-junction with two gates.

HUBBER-HOLME

MAP I2

2. Fork L (SSW) through LH gate (Note: when Pennine Bridleway is instated and signed you can go through RH gate for 1m/1.6km on track to T-junction at Old Ing.) and SO for 3.5m (5.5km) on bridleway – joining Pennine Way at T-junction at 0.4m (0.6km) and keeping L (SE) at track T-junction with Ribble Way at 2.5m (4km) – to staggered X-roads with B6479 and C-road. Turn R (N) onto C-road for 2.75m (4.4km) to High Birkwith then fork R (NE) for 0.4m (0.6km) on track to T-junction with signpost at Old Ing.

HIGH BIRKWITH

3. Turn L (N) for 4.5m (8km) on gated track – crossing Ling Gill Bridge at 1m (1.6km), mega-puddle at 1.5m (2.4km), turning R (ENE) at Cam End T-junction with signpost at 2.1m (3.4km) (4x4 erosion gets worse from here on) and keeping L (NE) at T-junction with C-road at 4m (6.4km) – to Cold Keld Gate. Go SO (ENE then E) for 2.9m (4.6km) – on gated unclassified road round Kidhow then keeping L (N) at T-junction at 2.5m (4km) – to T-junction with gated Cam High Road unclassified track. Fork R (NE) for 1.9m (3km) to bridleway T-junction (easy to overshoot; it's 0.2m/0.3km beyond sharp RH bend.)

CAM END

KIDHOW

MAP I3

4. Turn R (SE) for 1.4m (2.2km) – on rutty track, keeping L (E) at T-junction with waymarker at 0.2m (0.3km), swinging L/R (effectively SO) round shake hole immediately after 1st gate, through wall gap, going SO (ENE) at waymarkers at 0.5m (0.8km) and at 0.6m (1km) – to go through gate. Swing R (E) for 0.6m (1km) – down twisty, rubbly singletrack and

COUNTER-SETT

BUSK MOSS

MAP I1

swinging R/L at gate at 0.5m (0.8km) – to C-road. Turn R (E) for 3.6m (5.8km) (very steep and twisty with junction: take care!) – zigzagging R/L (effectively SO) (E) at staggered X-roads at 0.5m (0.8km) in Countersett, sharp RH bend after bridge, keeping R (SSW, towards Stalling Busk) at T-junction at 1m (1.6km) and forking L (S) onto High Lane track at 1.5m (2.4km) – to track T-junction with signpost on Busk Moss.

5. Keep R (SSE) for 2.6m (4.2km) – gets rougher and more technical from about 1.5m (2.4km) – to T-junction with B6160. Turn R (S) for 0.5m (0.8km) (steep! Your exit is just after sharp RH bend) to gated T-junction with bridleway. Turn L (SSE) for 1.75m (2.8km) – on muddy track, tricky ford at 0.4m (0.6km) then fast, loose descent after gate at 1m (1.6km) (walkers: watch your speed) – to start.

ROUTE J: PEN-Y-GHENT (SPORT)

MAPS J/K 1, J/K 2 (OS 98)
Distance: 18 miles (29km)
Height-gain: 1750ft (530m)
Time: 3.5hrs (dry), 5hrs (wet)
Navigation Skills: easy/moderate
Ride Direction: either way

A loop around one of the Dales most famous peaks, this Sport ride has hidden depths. Foxup Moor suffers from wet-soil erosion; please use an alternative loop if the ground's gloopy and please note that there's a mile or so of permissive track on Foxup Moor, it is not a right of way.

A big, big climb out of Littondale with a pernickety patch of loose stuff to circumnavigate at the outset, then it's unremitting granny ring to the top. Triple tough in the wet! With the Big climb of the day bagged, the best is yet to come. Downhilling begins in earnest soon after rounding Churn Milk Hole, where Experts often come to grief. If the ruts don't get you the loose stuff surely will!
From Helwith Bridge the road through Horton (café here) is

continued on page 60 ...

MAP 13 LANGSTROTHDALE CHASE

PEN-Y-GHENT; HORSE HEAD MAP J/K 1

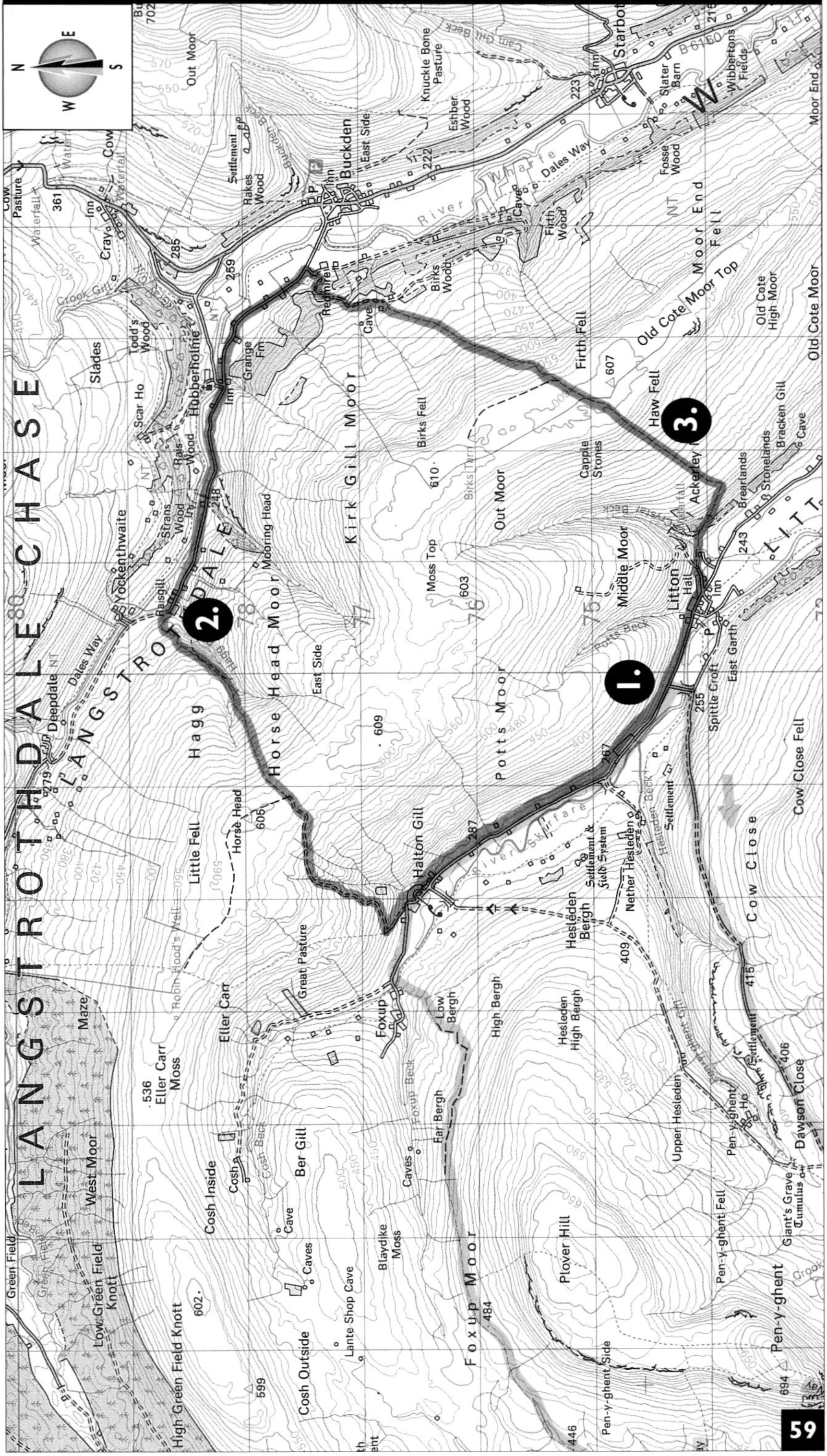

busy with juggernauts but you escape soon enough on a gritty climb up to Hull Pot and that's where semi-technical, fun-time singletracking begins. Much is unrideable in the wet so take heed of the caution already given. There's a couple of tricky dips and one, as you begin the descent down to Foxup, is endo-inducing.

NEW BRIDGE

MAP J/K 2

CHURN MILK HOLE

1. Start New Bridge (GR897742). Immediately after crossing River Skirfare on New Bridge turn R (W) for 3.2m (5.1km) – up track above Pen-y-Ghent Gill valley – to T-junction with C-road then turn L (S) for 1.2m (1.9km) to T-junction with unclassified county road (Pennine Way) by Dale Head farm. Turn R (NW) for 2.6m (4.2km) – on Pennine Way at first before turning L (SW) by Churn Milk Hole at T-junction at 0.6m (1km) onto Long Lane – to T-junction with B6479 (watch your speed: wheel-grabbing ruts, plus you'll overshoot onto main road!).

HORTON-IN-RIBBLESDALE

HULL POT

2. Turn R (NNE) for 2m (3.2km) to T-junction with Pennine Way bridleway track in Horton-in-Ribblesdale (75yds (70m) before Tourist Information Centre/café). Turn R (NE) for 1.75m (2.8km) up track to go through gate at track/singletrack X-roads. Go SO (NE) for 0.2m (0.3km) on singletrack – turning R (E) at 0.15m (0.25km) – to stile just before Hull Pot (easy to fall into in poor visibility!).

MAP J/K 1

FOXUP FARM

3. Cross stile, swing L (NE) for 2.6m (4.2km) – zigzagging L/R (effectively SO) (NE) on rocky track alongside wall at 0.3m (0.5km), zigzagging L/R (effectively SO) (E) by signpost at 2.5m (4km) onto track – to gate. Go SO (E) for 0.9m (1.4km) on permissive track with marker posts – forking L (ENE) at 0.6m (1km), tricky ford at 0.7m (1.15km), swinging L (NNE) at 0.8m (1.3km) – to go through gate. Swing L (NE) for 0.4m (0.6km) – joining bridleway and swinging L (N) just after gate at 0.2m (0.3km) – to Foxup Farm. Turn R (ENE) on C-road for 2.5m (4km) – keeping L (SE) at T-junction at 0.75m (1.2km) – to T-junction with track to New Bridge then turn R (SSW) to start.

ROUTE K: HORSE HEAD MOOR (SPORT)

MAPS J/K 1, J/K 2 (OS 98)
Distance: 12 miles (19km)
Height-gain: 2200ft (660m)
Time: 2.5hrs (dry), 4hrs (wet)
Navigation Skills: easy
Ride Direction: clockwise

Technically extreme this double up and down route is destined to test trail skills to the limit.

The road ride to Halton Gill, where the off-road kicks in with a killer climb, is almost too short. On the ascent take time to pick your line round the first RH bend then hit turbo-boost; if you clear that then you've a good chance of making a clean climb. Then it's a wild ride down to Yockenthwaite. Watch out for grass-covered trenches on the singletrack run-out to the road.

   Another gruelling climb takes you out of Wharfedale. Off the top the trail turns technical with steps, drop-offs to stretch your expertise. There are hidden drop-offs so curb the speed and the cobbly bit near the bottom is an ice-rink in the wet.

NEW BRIDGE
1. Start New Bridge (GR897742). At T-junction with C-road turn L (WNW) for 2m (3.2km) – through Halton Gill – to T-junction with gated unclassified track. Fork R (NW then NE, signed Hawes) for 2.6m (4.2km) – going SO (NE) at **HORSE HEAD** Horse Head gate onto bridleway at 1.25m (2km), tricky descent starting at 1.5m (2.4km) and **LANG-** bridleway swinging R (ESE) for last 140yds (125m **STROTH-** – to C-road in Langstrothdale. **DALE**

2. Turn R (S then ESE) for 2.2m (3.5km) – keeping R (ESE) at T-junction just before bridge at 1.25m (2km) – to T-junction with bridleway track. Turn R (SW) for 2.1m (3.4km) – turning R (SW) at signed T-junction at 0.7m (1.15km) and almost immediately going SO (SW then SSW) track X-roads onto singletrack with marker posts (boggy in places) and swinging L (SSW) through gap in wall at 1.8m **FIRTH FELL** (2.9km) – to go through gate on Firth Fell summit.

N
W E
S

Cross Pot
Top Fm
Fawber
Horton Moor
Hull Pot
Pot Hole
Pen-y-ghent Side
Sell Gill Holes
3.
P Way
Upper
Hunt Pot
Pennine Way
394
Pen-y-ghent Fell
Pen-
252
New Houses
Harber
Scar
Harber
239
Horton Scar
694
Pen-y-ghent
Giant's Grave
Tumulus
Daw
Brants
Gill Head
Penyghent
Pot
Beecroft
Hall
Inn
Horton in Ribblesdale
P
Sch
Brackenbottom
Fawcett
Moor
Blishmire Ho
Blishmire
Close
Cattle
Grid
In
436
Moughton
Gavel
Rigg
Larch Tree
Hole
Rainscar
Pennine Way
Dry
Beck
Dub Cote Scar
Churn Milk Hole
433
Dale Head
424
Dub Cote
Newland
Ho
Cattle Grid
Rainscar
New Pasture
Cragghill
Fm
399
Cairn
Overdale
F O
Arcow
Quarry
81
82
338
83
84
Silverdale
85
4
Scar
Studfold
Gingling Hole
Coa
Wks
234
440
Coronati
Foredale
Ribble Way
Silverdale
Barn
Pot Holes
Out
Moughton
Far End
Nab
Dry Rigg
Quarry
Inn
420
Pot Holes
06
226
2.
Bridge
400
Neals Ing
Bark
Houses
Swarth
Moor
Sherwood Ho
Sannat Hall Fm
Bergh Ho
Rough Close
Settlement
Billinger
Barns
Catrigg
Westside Ho
Smearsett Scar
363
229
201
Stainforth
407
Feizor
Enclosure
Little
Stainforth
Stainforth
Dead Man's
Cave
67
Catrigg Force
370
Cowside Beck
400
unton Ho
66
Upper Winskill
Cowside
Daw Haw
ave Hole
Cairns
Borrins
Wood
Ribble Way
Winskill
Stones
368
Overclose
420
Giggleswick
Caves
Kinsey Cave
Mill
Jubilee Cave
Langcliffe Scar
Buck Haw Brow
201
Caves
Stackhouse
Weir
Cave
Victoria Cave
Huntworth
65
Caves
Cairn
Langcliffe
Place
Clay Pits
Plantation
Cave
516
Settle
Scar
253
High Paley
Green
Croft
Closes
Catteral
Hall
Sch
147
Mill
Langcliffe
Attermire
Scar
440
Cave
Attermire Cave
Low Barn
369
Stockdale
Fm
Weir
64
Hospt
484
Gigglewick
Close Ho
SETTLE
398
Sugar Loaf
Hill
Cave
GIGGLESWICK STA
PH
296
Grain Ho
Field Gate
Hotel
Swaw Beck
Gildersleets
Anley
Ho
Weir
Scaleber
Force
Sewage Wks
Black's Plantn
lebank

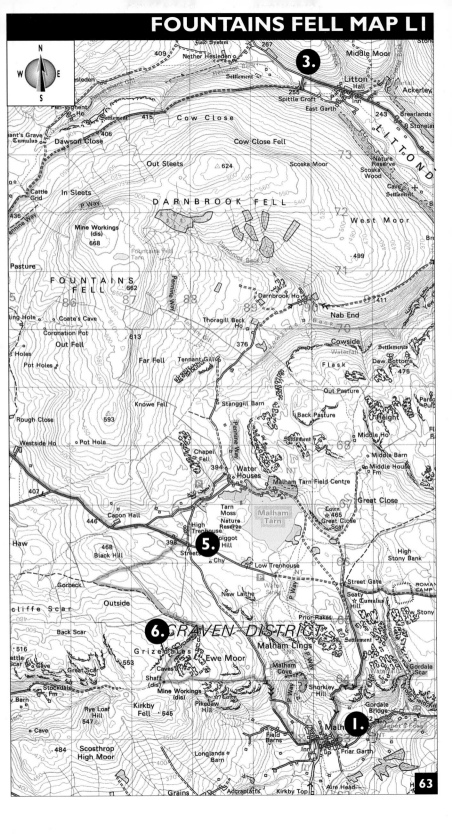

3. Go SO (SW) for 1.25m (2km) – keeping near wall on technical singletrack with drop-offs starting at 0.2m (0.3km), zigzagging L/R (effectively SO) (SSE then W) around edge at 0.8m (1.3km) then down rough gated track – to go through field gate. Swing L (W) for 1m (1.6km) – turning R (WNW) at T-junction with C-road in Litton at 0.3m (0.5km) – to track T-junction near New Bridge. Turn L (SSW) to start.

LITTON

MALHAM MOORS

ROUTE L: FOUNTAINS FELL (EXPERT)

MAPS L1, L2 & L3 (OS 98)
Distance: 33 miles (53km)
Height-gain: 3300ft (1000m)
Time: 5hrs (dry), 7hrs (wet)
Navigation Skills: moderate/difficult
Ride Direction: anti-clockwise

Grand tour through gorgeous terrain that finishes with a 1000ft (300m) downhill fling for a finale.

The first off-road leg to Kilnsey is along the infamous Mastiles Lane. Keep to the centre trenches even though they look the least inviting; top-stones lurk in the turf ready to unseat the unwary rider. Some folk really rate the descent off Kilnsey Moor; it may be fast but that's about it. We take a short detour to take in a descent with more character – Green Haw Hill.

From Kilnsey it's a tarmac excursion up Littondale – reckoned by many to be the Dales most picturesque valley – to New Bridge. The starting point for Sport Route J which we follow almost all the way to Helwith Bridge. Once on Moor Head Lane it's a testing climb in the wet to the top for a roller-coaster road ride to Streets crossroads. This is where navigation skills are tested – sometimes the singletrack's a little vague but follow the directions and you should stay on track to Gorbeck's boggy by-way. We zigzag all the way to the top of Grizedales for some gratuitous downhilling all the way home. Watch for the slip in the wet and things get a touch rocky on the chicanes to the lane.

MALHAM

STREET GATE

MAP L2

HOWGILL

1. Start Malham Bridge (GR901629). Head uphill past YHA (NE, towards Malham Tarn) for 2m (3.2km) to then fork R (NNW) for 0.2m (0.3km) on track to gate. Turn R (ESE) through Street Gate for 2.2m (3.5km) – alongside wall on your R – to T-junction with bridleway just after gate. Turn R (ESE) for 1.5m (2.4km) – going SO (ESE) bridleway/C-road X-roads at 0.6m (1km) – to X-roads with gated bridleway. Turn L (NE) for 1.5m (2.4km) – through zigzag R/L (effectively SO) then heading N following marker posts, gate at 0.5m (0.8km), keeping L at T-junction at 0.75m (1.2km) and keeping R at vague T-junction at 1.25m (2km) – to T-junction with Mastiles track at Howgill.

KILNSEY

MAP L1

LITTON

NEW BRIDGE

2. Turn R (ENE) for 1m (1.6km) – over Cool spur and keeping R at T-junctions at 0.25m (0.4km) and 0.6m (1km) – to T-junction with B6160 in Kilnsey. Turn L (N) for 1m (1.6km) – past Kilnsey Crag and over Skirfare Bridge – to T-junction and then turn L (NW) over cattle grid for 6.4m (10.2km) – up Littondale passing through Hawkswick (tea room here.), by Arncliffe, through Litton and turning L (SSW) at T-junction with unclassified county track at 6.2m (10km) – to gated T-junction immediately after crossing River Skirfare on New Bridge.

MAP L3

CHURN MILK HOLE

3. Turn R (W) for 3.2m (5.1km) – up track above Pen-y-Ghent Gill valley – to T-junction with C-road then turn L (S) for 1.2m (2km) to T-junction with unclassified county road (Pennine Way) by Dale Head farm. Turn R (NW) for 0.6m (1km) to T-junction by Churn Milk Hole then turn L (SW) for 2m (3.2km) along Long Lane down to obvious track T-junction (watch your speed or you'll overshoot!).

SANNAT HALL

4. Turn L (ESE) for 1.5m (2.4km) on roller-coaster Moor Head Lane bridleway/unclassified county track to C-road. Turn L (NE) for 0.12m (0.2km) to T-junction then turn R (ESE, towards Malham) for 3m (4.8km) – through deep valley by Sannat Hall and SO (ESE) at next T-junction – to T-junction on LH bend. Go SO (ESE) over cattle grid for 0.5m (0.8km) to X-roads.

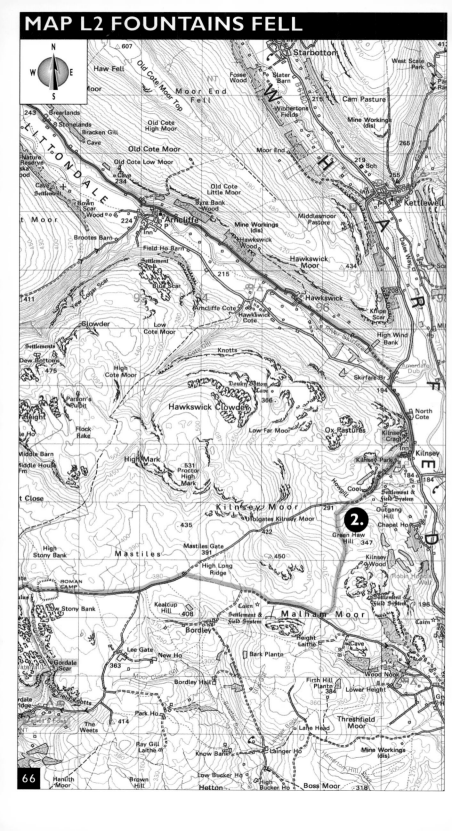

N
W E
S

Cross Pot
Horton Moor
Pen-y-ghent Side
Top Fm
Fawber
Hull Pot
Pot Hole
Sell Gill Holes
P Way
Upper
Pennine Way
Hunt Pot
Pen-y-ghent Fell
Pen-y
394
Penyghent Pot
694
Pen-y-ghent
Giant's Grave
Tumulus
Daw
252
New Houses
Harber Scar
Horton Scar
Blishmire Ho
239
Brants Gill Head
Harber
Blishmire Close
Cattle Grid
In
Horton in Ribblesdale
Gavel Rigg
Fawcett Moor
Rainscar
436
Beecroft Hall
Sch
Brackenbottom
Larch Tree
Churn Milk Hole
433
424
Works
Dub Cote Scar
Hole
Dale Head
P Way
Pennine Way
Moughton
Dry Beck
Dub Cote
Cattle Grid
Rainscar
New Pasture
Newland Ho
Cairn
399
Overdale
F O
Cragghill Fm
Arcow Quarry
81
82
338
83
84
85
8
Scar
Studfold
Silverdale
Gingling Hole
Coa
Wks
234
440
Coronation
Foredale
420
Out
Moughton Far End
Nab
Dry Rigg Quarry
Inn
4.
Ribble Way
Silverdale Barn
Pot Holes
Pot Holes
06
226
Helwith Bridge
400
Neals Ing
Bark Houses
Swarth Moor
Sherwood Ho
440
Sannat Hall Fm
Rough Close
Bargh Ho
Westside Ho
Settlement
Smearsett Scar
363
Billinger Barns
Catrigg
229
201
407
Enclosure
Little Stainforth
Stainforth
Dead Man's Cave
Stainforth
Catrigg Force
Cowside Beck
Taitlands
Upper Winskill
Cowside
Daw Haw
unton Ho
Cairns
Borrins Wood
Winskill Stones
368
ve Hole
66
Mill
Overclose
380
Kinsey Cave
Caves
B 6480
Buck Haw Brow
201
Stackhouse
Weir
Jubilee Cave
Gorb
Huntworth
Caves
Langcliffe Place
Cave
Victoria Cave
Langcliffe Scar
65
MS
Mill
480
High Paley Green
CH
Langcliffe
Clay Pits Plantation
Cave
Back
Croft Closes
Cairn
500
516
Catteral Hall Sch
470
Weir
440
Attermire
Settle Scar
Cave
64
Cave
Aftermire Cave
Hospl
369
Stockdale Fm
Giggleswick
Close Ho
SETTLE
398
Low Barn
Cave
GIGGLESWICK STA
Sugar Loaf Hill
Grain Ho
Field Gate
PH
Hotel
296
484
Swaw Beck
Gildersleets
Anley Weir
Scalebert Force
Littlebank
Sewage Wks
Black's Plantn

MAP LI

5. Take hairpin turn R (W) for 0.1m (0.15km) – on very feint bridleway across field – to gate then swing L (SW then WSW) for 0.5m (0.8km) – on bridleway singletrack (don't wander off line on sheep trails.), over stream, past marker-post and on up singletrack – to bridleway gate. Go SO (W) for 0.3m (0.5km) – beside broken wall at first then swinging L (WSW) just before field corner to cross another broken

BLACK HILL

wall and over Black Hill col on singletrack that does a lazy R/L swing for final 220yds (200m) – to gate. Go SO (W then WSW) for 0.4m (0.6km) on bridleway to T-junction with unclassified county grass track (about 110yds/100m E of a gate) then turn L (ESE) for 0.9m (1.4km) climb up to two gates.

6. Go through RH gate and continue (ESE) for 0.5m (0.8km) down track to turn R (SW) just before gate then climb for 0.8m (1.3km) – on obvious bridleway

GRIZEDALES

over Grizedales through three gates then up to and alongside wall – to T-junction with track by gate. Turn L (E) for 1.25m (2km) descent – track zigzags near the bottom – to gate on C-road into Malham. Turn R (SSE) for 0.2m (0.3km) (keep your speed in check) to LH bend then go SO (S) through gate for 0.8m (1.3km) – on feint bridleway across field at first then on walled lane – to track T-junction in

MALHAM

Malham then turn L (N then NE) for 0.12m (0.2km) to C-road in Malham and turn R (S) to start.

ROUTE M: LANGCLIFFE SCAR (SPORT)

MAP M1 (OS 98)
Distance: 14 miles (22km)
Height-gain: 2160ft (655m)
Time: 2.5hrs (dry), 3.5hrs (wet)
Navigation Skills: moderate
Ride Direction: either way

Slippery when wet, it's a slick rock limestone loop with 800ft (250m) of gravity-suck to close the circuit.

Malham's a pretty place but all the moorland routes are up. 1000ft (300m) of up. Happily half that's on tarmac and that gives a good view of the spectacular Cove cliffs. The descent to Stockdale's an interesting exercise in 'skip 'n slip' when wet – and it usually is – then it's a mix of tarmac and muddy track all the way into Settle. Followed by a rocky climb to fields where clay singletrack contours its way past Clay Pits Plantation to the road. But we touch tarmac only briefly. Onwards and upwards on ancient by-way that, before too long, goes in for some big-time bog-trotting. Negotiating this road's dark, peaty pools is a lottery. One barely wets your tread, the next immediately engulfs the front wheel and it's endo time! If it's dry it's a doddle. After that the run down to Malham's pure fun.

MALHAM

1. Start Malham Bridge (GR901629). At T-junction in front of the Buck Inn turn R (NNW) for 1m (1.6km) climb to gate with bridleway signpost then turn L (W) for 2.6m (4.2km) – climbing up obvious gated track (it zigzags a bit at first) past footpath signpost and over Kirkby Fell col – to join Stockdale farm drive. Turn right (WSW) for 1.3m (2.1km) to C-road T-junction then turn R (W, towards Settle) for 110yds (100m) to then turn L (S) for 1.3m (2.1km) – onto bridleway track past Blacks Plantation, keeping right at the next two T-junctions – to T-junction with C-road.

KIRBY FELL

BLACK'S PLANTA-TION

SETTLE

2. Turn L (WSW) for 0.5m (0.8km) – skirting Settle village and keeping R at all T-junctions – to T-junction with unclassified county track then fork R (NE) for 0.75m (1.2km) – up walled track then contouring (N) in field, then between walls again and out alongside field boundary – to gate. Go through and immediately swing R (NE) for 0.5m (0.8km) – feint grass singletrack becomes obvious after 220yds (200m) then on gated singletrack past woods – to gate onto C-road.

VICTORIA CAVE

3. Go through and turn R (ESE) for 80yds (75m) to T-junction with unclassified county road and keep SO (ESE then ENE) for 1.8m (2.9km) – on obvious track past Victoria Cave, over col then swinging R (E) alongside boundary wall when gravel gives way to grass – to stream crossing. Swing R (E)

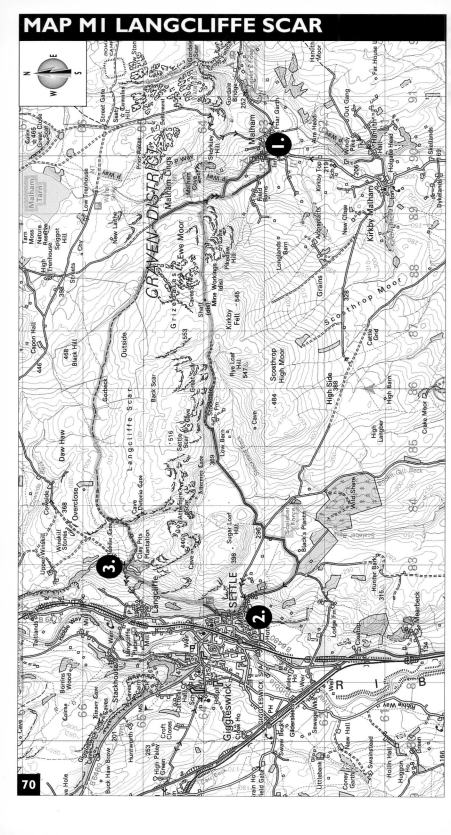

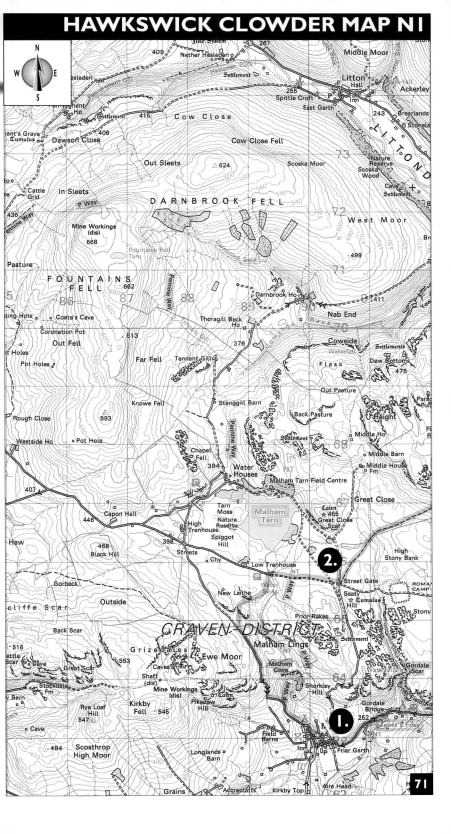

GORBECK

for 1.75m (2.8km) – on obvious, boggy roller-coaster moorland track around Gorbeck that gradually swings R (SE) – finally climbing to two gates. Go through RH gate and continue (ESE) for 1m (1.6km) down gated track to C-road then turn R (SSE) for 0.8m (1.3km) (keep your speed in check) to LH bend then go SO (S) through gate for 0.8m (1.3km) – on feint bridleway across field at first then on walled lane – to track T-junction in Malham then turn L (N then NE) for 0.12m (0.2km) to C-road in Malham and turn R (S) to start.

ROUTE N: HAWKSWICK CLOWDER (SPORT)

MAPS N1 & N2 (OS 98)
Distance: 16 miles (26km)
Height-gain: 2350ft (710m)
Time: 2.5hrs (dry), 3.5hrs (wet)
Navigation Skills: moderate
Ride Direction: clockwise

A tad tough for newcomers, but the technical quotient's low; the scenics sumptuous.

The Malham valley makes a stunning backdrop as you climb up to Street Gate to pick up the unclassified track to Arncliffe Cote (This road may be down-graded to bridleway in the future.). In the mist navigation can be a bit tricky in places but, follow the directions carefully, and you'll be OK. If it's clear Wharfedale's amazing limestone crags come into view as you crest Flock Rake then it's the twisting, mostly grass, descent to Arncote to enjoy – slippery when wet.

The return leg to Malham makes use of another ancient road – Mastiles Lane. It was surfaced all the way but recent adoption by powered vehicles has churned the top-most section to quagmire. This loop avoids the gloop, but it's still testing. The last haul up over Kilnsey Moor is a physically demanding and mentally intimidating climb – more so when those limestone 'cobbles' have a lick of water on them. Watch your speed on the drive into Bordley and again on the lanes to Malham. If you've time take a look at Gordale Scar – it's an astonishing sight.

MALHAM

1. Start Malham Bridge (GR901629). At T-junction in front of the Buck Inn turn R (NNW) for 1.7m (2.7km) to signposted bridleway just over cattle grid and immediately fork R (N) onto signposted bridleway track for 0.25m (0.4km) to turn R (ENE) through gate then SO (ENE) for

MALHAM TARN

0.6m (1km) down obvious bridleway that swings L (N) to C-road by Malham Tarn. Turn R (E) for 0.8m (1.3km) to go SO (E) at crossroads with unclassified county tracks to Street Gate.

MAP N2

2. Go through gate then fork L (NNE) onto High Cote Lane unclassified county track for 0.6m (1km) – swinging L (N) at 0.5m (0.8km) – to go through gate. Continue (N) for 0.1m (0.15km) – up Gordale Beck at first – to then turn R (E) for 0.8m (1.3km) – green track vague at first – up to gate. Go through gate then swing L (NNE) for 0.12m (0.2km) down to another gate. Continue

HIGH MARK

(NNE) for 0.5m (0.8km) – over High Mark col, keeping R (NE) by waymarker – to gate.

3. Go through then swing L (NE) for 0.4m (0.6km) – keeping alongside broken wall then through another gate – to waymarker at top of descent then turn L (WNW) for 0.25m (0.4km) – soon swinging R (NE) – drop to gate. Go through and continue SO (NE) for 1.1m (1.76km) – through ford/gate/ ford combo – to go through another gate to then swing L (NNE then ENE) for 0.75m (1.2km) – down spur then through hairpin bends – to yet another

ARNCLIFFE COTE FARM

gate. Go SO (NE) for 0.2m (0.3km) – past Arncliffe Cote Farm (please take extra care; this RoW is under threat) – to T-junction with C-road.

4. Turn R (SE) for 1.9m (3km) to T-junction with B6160 then keep R (SE and effectively SO) for

KILNSEY

0.8m (1.3km) – past Kilnsey Crag – to Kilnsey then turn R (W) just past the Tennant Arms for 0.4m (0.6km) – up tarmac lane, past Old Kilnsey Hall – to signposted T-junction with Mastiles Lane unclassified county track. Fork L (SW) for 2m

MASTILES GATE

(3.2km) – over Kilnsey Moor – to Mastiles Gate T-junction.

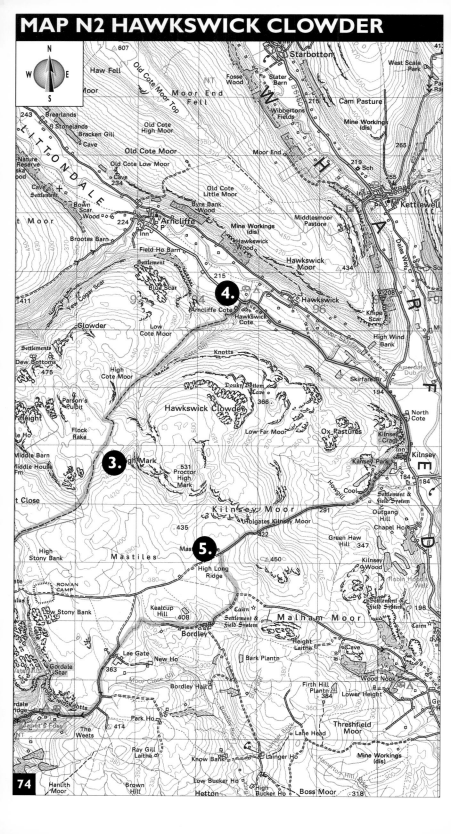

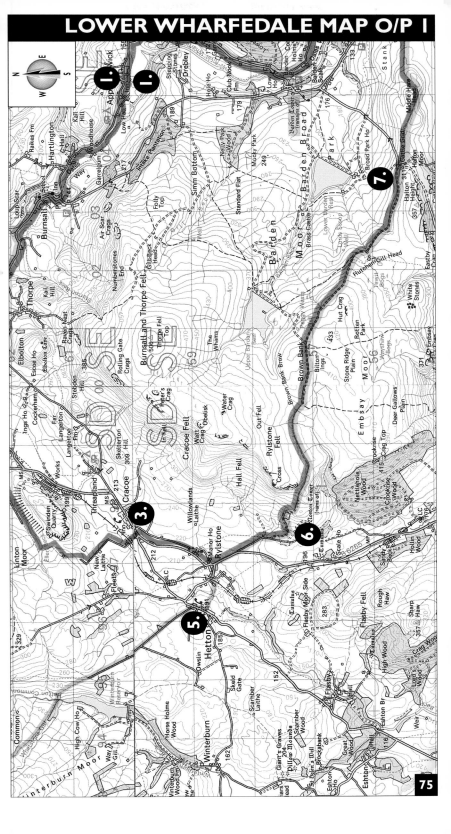

BORDLEY GREEN FARM

5. Turn L (S) for 1.1m (1.75km) on bridleway – SO (SW) gated X-roads at 0.5m (0.8km) – to Bordley Green Farm (last bit into farmyard is steep, please ride slowly). Zigzag R/L (Following bridleway signpost to continue W; effectively SO) through yard for 0.5m (0.8km) – on obvious bridleway track that swings R across field corner – to go through gate. Zigzag R/L (effectively SW) for

LEE GATE

0.7m (1.15km) – first crossing little valley – to Lee Gate farm gate then turn R for 140yds (125m) to T-junction and turn L for 2.2m (3.5km) – joining C-road past Gordale Scar and Janet's Foss

MAP N1

waterfall – to T-junction above Malham then go SO (W) for 0.25m (0.4km) down to the start.

LOWER WHARFEDALE

ROUTE O: HETTON AND BARDEN MOORS (EXPERT)

MAPS O/P 1, O/P 2, O/P 3
(OS 98, 103 & 104)
Distance: 32 miles (51km)
Height-gain: 3355ft (1015m)
Time: 4.5hrs (dry), 5.5hrs (wet)
Navigation Skills: easy/moderate
Ride Direction: anti-clockwise

A pot-pourri of Dale trails; a delight to ride whatever the weather with a 4m (6.5km) descent to endure (Not!).

A nice tarmac warm-up on the **Wharfedale** road before cutting to granny-cog on the climb over **Threshfield Moor**. But if you thought that track was a technical teaser then be prepared for the bog-snatchers that follow. They've been known to swallow a quad bike! A touch of green lane at **Height Laithe**, bounded by a medley of crumbling walls and neat stone barn, is a summary of the Dales condensed into an acre of landscape.

Beyond **Bordley** white tracks cut across deep, green pastures where we join the lane to Lee Gate for a short interlude of tyre-hum interlude then it's back to track (Easy to over-shoot the junction.) for the climb onto The Weets. Grassy singletrack dips down to the head of Winterburn Reservoir but its benign nature hides a few drop-ins – or 'fly-outs' if you prefer! The neat little bridge marks the start of a short, sharp technical climb that delivers you to the top of the big-ring run down to Hetton. Hetton Beck's spanned by a bizarre stone – as in one big rock – bridge that looks distinctly second-hand.

Beware of the traffic on the B6265 – more quarry lorries. Rylstone Ridge, it's craggy cliffs topped by a gaunt cross, lies ahead and marks the last big climb of the day. The old bridleway was up twisting singletrack, but the new one may well follow the less testing shooting track. Hard work all the same! Out on the top it's a sea-change from limestone and lush pastures to gritstone and grouse moor. A short section of techno-track is cut off in its prime with path erosion control. Underneath lurks mega-bog so it's not as bad as it seems. Then as sweeping vistas over Embsay Moor open up, the track takes a downward trend. For miles. All big-ring spinning as you high-tail it for the road at Halton Height. Shooting track gives way to green bridleway over Middle Hare Head – beware of the bog as you drop off the hill, into the woods and off down to Bolton's Pavilion for a well-earned cuppa. (The route through the valley here is permissive to users of MTB-Pro guides only.)

APPLETREE-WICK

MAP O/P 2

THRESH-FIELD MOOR

1. Start New Inn (ask in pub about secure parking) in Appletreewick (GR 052601) and turn R (W) for 4.9m (7.8km) – turning R (NW) onto B6160 at Burnsall at 1.6m (2.6km), forking L (W) off B-road at 4.7m (7.5km) into Threshfield – to T-junction with B6265. Turn L (SSW) for 1m (1.6km) – turning R (W) (busy road: take care!) at T-junction with unclassified road at 0.2m (0.3km), keeping SO (W) at T-junction at 0.7m (1.15km) – to gate onto Threshfield Moor.

MALHAM MOOR

2. Turn R (WNW, SW then W) for 1m (1.6km) – keeping L at T-junctions at 0.1m (0.15km) and at 0.4m (0.6km) – to T-junction with singletrack bridleway by waymarker then fork L (W) for 1m (1.6km) – turning R (NNW) at T-junction with waymarker at 0.25m (0.4km) – along track to gate onto Malham Moor. Go SO (N) for 1m (1.6km) – boggy singletrack, follow marker posts; there's a green lane interlude at Height Laithe – to C-road.

MAP O/P 2 LOWER WHARFEDALE

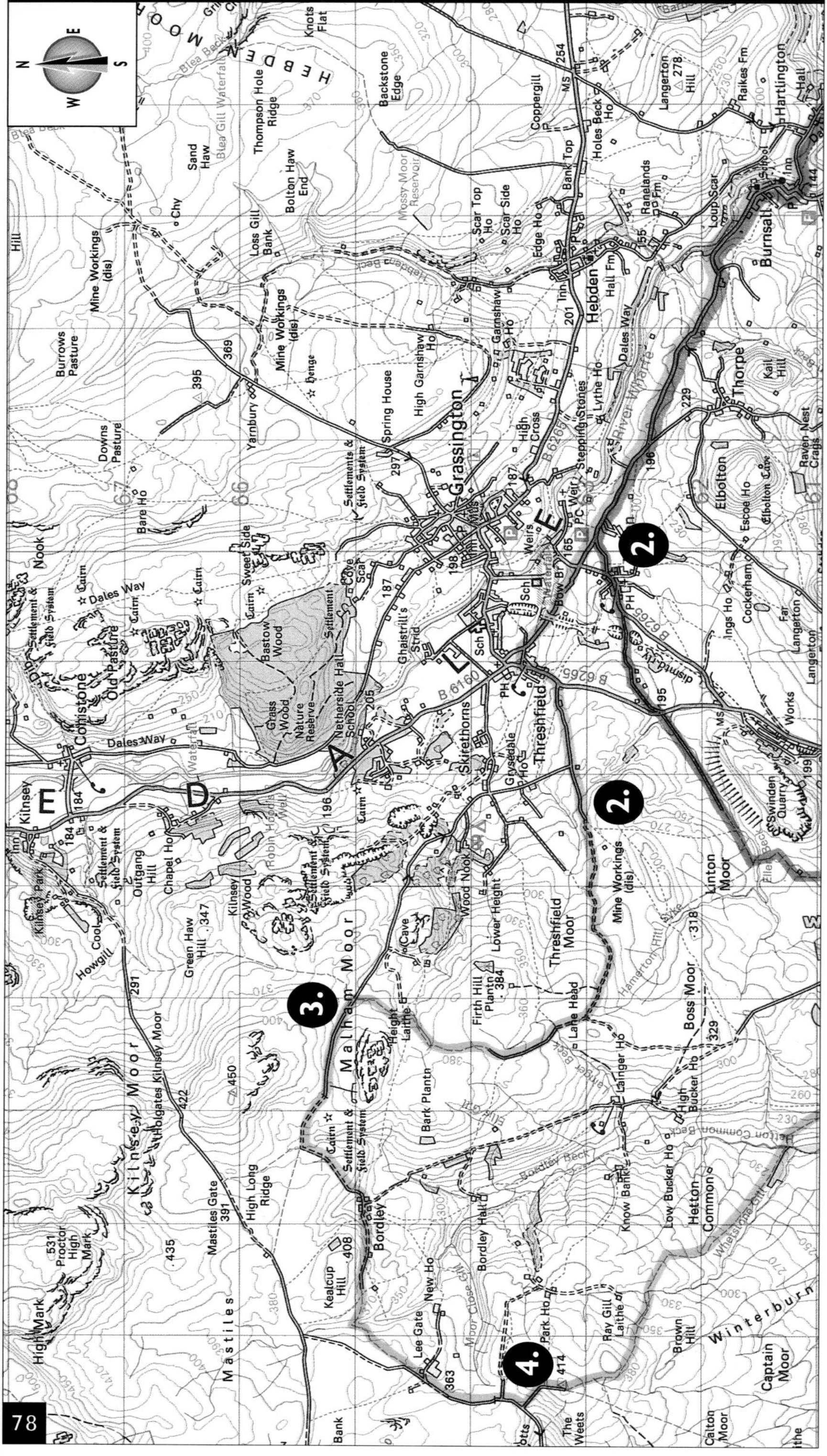

BORDLEY GREEN FARM

3. Turn L (WNW) for 1.5m (2.4km) – turning L (SW) at gated X-roads at 0.9m (1.4km) – to Bordley Green Farm (last bit into farmyard is steep, please ride slowly). Cross to far R corner of yard then go through gate into fields. Go through gate (WSW) on track for 1.2m (1.9km) – swinging R (WNW, away from wall) at 0.5m (0.8km) then zigzagging R/L (effectively SW) across valley after

LEE GATE

gate at 0.7m (1.15km) – to farm at Lee Gate then turn R (WNW) for 0.75m (1.2km) – turning L (SW) at T-junction at 80yds (75m) – to T-junction with bridleway track just over brow of hill (easy to miss; signpost obscured by wall).

THE WEETS

4. Turn L (SE, signed Calton) for 0.3m (0.5km) – through gate – up to bridleway T-junction near trig point on The Weets. Keep L (SSE, signed Hetton) on singletrack for 0.3m (0.5km) to go through gate then swing R (S then SE) for 1.8m (2.9km) – round hill top, tricky dip at 0.6m (1km) then turning R (S then SE) at gate at 0.9m (1.4km) – to bridge above Winterburn Reservoir. Cross bridge then continue for 0.5m (0.8km) – up L/R zigzag (effectively SO) then swinging L (SE) – up to gated bridleway X-roads then go SO (SSE) for 1.4m (2.2km) to

MAP O/P 1

HETTON

T-junction with C-road in Hetton.

RYLSTONE

5. Turn R (SSW) for 0.75m (1.2km) – turning L (ESE) onto bridleway track at 0.15m (0.25km), joining drive at 0.6m (1km) – to T-junction with C-road then turn R (ESE) for 0.2m (0.3km) – immediately under railway – to T-junction with B6265 in Rylstone (busy road; take care). Turn R (SSE) for 0.75m (1.2km) – turning L (E then SSE) onto bridleway track at 0.25m (0.4km) – to gated bridleway T-junction.

6. Next bit of bridleway is vague and is destined to be re-routed onto track 100yds (90m) N but for now turn L (E), through gate, for 0.8m (1.3km) – turning R (S) on 'track' at 100yds (90m) and turning L (E) up singletrack at 2nd telegraph pole at 0.15m (0.25km), passing just to R of trees, then turning R (SE then E) at T-junction with obvious

EMBSAY MOOR

track at 0.5m (0.8km), SO gate at 0.6m (1km) – to gate onto Embsay Moor. Go SO (ESE) (random blue spots mark the route) for 1.7m (2.7km) – passing through wall at 0.12m (0.2km) and joining track at T-junction at 1m (1.6km) – to track T-junction 100yds (90m) beyond waymarker on Brown Bank. Keep R (ESE) for 2.3m (3.7km) –

HALTON MOOR

forking R (ESE) up onto T-junction with singletrack at 2m (3.2km) – to C-road at Halton Moor.

MAP O/P 3

7. Turn L (NW) for 0.12m (0.2km) – over cattle grid, just – to T-junction with gated bridleway then turn R (ESE) for 1.5m (2.4km) – through gate at 0.4m (0.6km), mega-bog at 1m (1.6km) – to field gate then fork R (SE) for 0.75m (1.2km) – SO (SE) X-roads at 0.2m (0.3km), through gate at 0.4m (0.6km) – to gate into wood. Go SO (E) for 0.5m (0.8km) – obvious bridleway (slippery when wet); turning R (SSW) at T-junction at 50yds (45m), forking L (SSE) at T-junction at 0.1m (0.15km), taking hairpin turn R at T-junction at 0.3m (0.5km) then exits woods – to pair of gates. Go through LH gate (SE then S) for 0.25m (0.4km) – swinging R to join track at 0.15m (0.25km) – to B6160 in

BOLTON

Bolton.

8. Turn L (NE) for 0.3m (0.5km) to T-junction by fountain then turn R (NE), leaving B-road, for 0.7m (1.15km) – turning R (NE) over bridge (please walk) at 0.5m (0.8km) opposite Pavilion Tea Rooms (open all summer and WEs in winter) – to T-junction with C-road. Turn L (NW) for 4.4m (7km) roller-coaster run – forking R (NNE) at T-junction at 2.4m (3.8km) and turning L (W) at T-junction at 4.0m (6.4km) – to start.

ROUTE P: CRACOE FELL (SPORT)

MAPS O/P 1, O/P 2, O/P 3
(OS 98, 103 & 104)
Distance: 22 miles (35km)
Height-gain: 1700ft (515m)
Time: 3hrs (dry), 3.5hrs (wet)
Navigation Skills: easy
Ride Direction: either way

Ideal winter's afternoon out with the option of a WE tea stop.

Essentially a short-cut option on the longer Route P, this loop is for those with limited experience but eager to exercise their new-won skills. Follow directions carefully as you make your way through Linton Moor.

APPLETREE-WICK

MAP O/P 2

1. Start New Inn (ask in pub about secure parking) in Appletreewick (GR 052601) and turn R (W) for 4.5m (7.2km) – turning R (NW) onto B6160 at Burnsall at 1.6m (2.6km), forking L (W) off B-road to Linton at T-junction at 4.0m (6.4km) and forking L (SW) onto B6265 at T-junction at 4.25m (6.8km) – to T-junction with bridleway just after Linton.

MAP O/P 1

2. Fork R (W) for 0.7m (1.15km) to drop down to X-roads with B6265 (busy road!) then go SO (SW) for 1.1m (1.8km) to bridleway T-junction (vague) then turn L (S) for 0.5m (0.8km) – through ford, passing to L of trees, don't go through gate at 0.25m (0.4km) and then keeping R of barn – to gate in field corner. Go SO (SW then SE) for 0.8m (1.3km) to track/road X-roads near Cracoe.

CRACOE

3. Turn L (ENE) for 0.1m (0.15km) on B6265 towards Cracoe then turn R (S) onto bridleway track for 1m (1.6km) – keeping L (S) at T-junction at 0.6m (1km) then keeping L around farm and church – to T-junction with B6265 in Rylstone. Turn L (SSE) for 0.25m (0.4km) to T-junction with bridleway track then turn L (E then SSE) for 0.5m (0.8km) to bridleway gate. Follow Route O from para No 6.

RYLSTONE

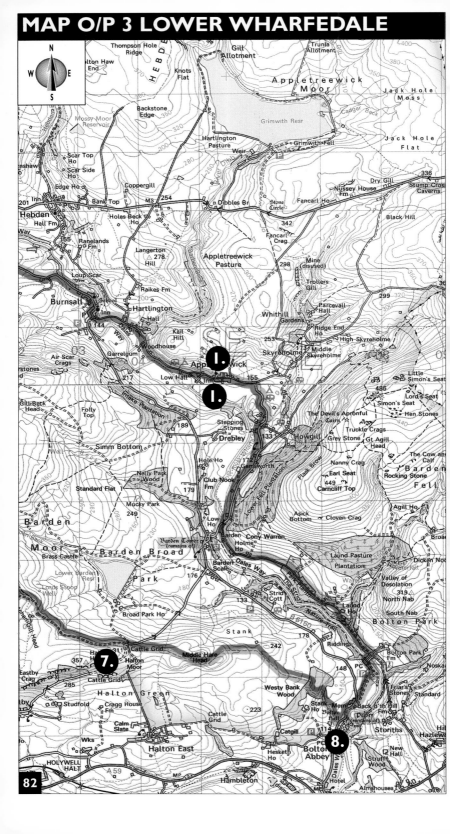

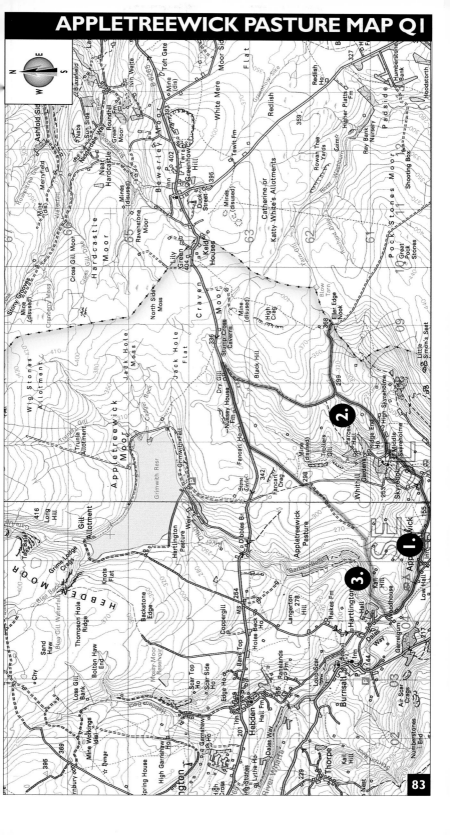

ROUTE Q: APPLETREEWICK PASTURE (FUN)

 MAP Q1 (OS 98 & 99)
Distance: 8 miles (13km)
Height-gain: 900ft (275m)
Time: 1hr (dry), 1.5hrs (wet)
Navigation Skills: easy
Ride Direction: anti-clockwise

Sweet little intro to Dale trails; a pub-to-pub evening saunter with scenics to savour. Made-to-measure night ride.

Always a delight to ride, this little loop kicks off with tarmac to stretch those city-stiff legs before tackling the only climb; up onto Eller Edge. The optional leg is well worth doing – especially if you're an up-and-coming descender, but watch out for the rut and rubble when you return. On the final descent from Appletreewick Pasture beware of those grass chicanes – in the wet they're slippery!

APPLETREE-WICK

1. Start New Inn (ask in pub about secure parking) in Appletreewick (GR 052601) and turn L (E) for 2.2m (3.5km) – keeping SO (E) at T-junction at 0.5m (0.8km), forking R (ESE) at T-junction at 0.7m (1.15km) and turning R (E) at T-junction at 1.25m (2km) – to track T-junction.

DRY GILL

2. Turn R (ENE) for 0.8m (1.3km) up to gate – take in views – then return to T-junction (don't forget the rough stuff near the bottom!) then turn R (NE, NW then NNW) for 1.5m (2.4km) to B6265 at Dry Gill. Turn L (WSW) for 1.75m (2.8km) – turning L (SSW) off B-road at 1st T-junction at 1m (1.6km) – to gated bridleway track just after LH bend then turn R (SW) for 1.25m (2km) – keeping SO at T-junction at 1m (1.6km) – to gated T-junction by buildings.

3. Turn R (W) for 0.6m (1km) – on grassy trail at first (ride carefully – sheep) then rubbly for the last 100yds (90m) – to C-road then turn L (S) for 1m (1.6km) back to start.

COVERDALE

ROUTE R: THE WHERNSIDES (EXPERT)

MAPS R/S 1, R/S 2 (OS 98 & 99)
Height-gain: 3800ft (1150m)
Time: 6.5hrs (dry), 9hrs (wet)
Navigation Skills: moderate/difficult
Ride Direction: clockwise (dry), anti-clockwise (wet)
Distance: 25m (40km)

A full day out on the fells; not for the faint-hearted. It's gruelling in the wet so wait for a dry spell before tackling this scenic roller-coaster.

The climb over the Whernsides is sodden singletrack so if it's wet take the track over Arkleside instead. Even in the dry, the adverse gradient will reduce all but the toughest riders to jelly. And the map's a tad optimistic when it classes the decreasing contour values to Coverdale Head as 'downhill' – the muddy path plummets into boggy ravines at regular intervals.

From Coverdale the route contour trots above Wharfedale – the views are sumptuous, the track entertaining. A stiff climb over the shoulders of Buckden Pike then the bridleway plunges down steep, sometimes boggy, singletrack to Walden Head. The area's peppered with grass-covered grykes so watch out, and there's a hidden step right on the lip of the last, steep drop. From the fords – two becks converge here – a new bridleway route may be in place; follow YDNP signs to pick up the lane.

The climb up from Cote is a killer. The gradient increases as you go, and just the track kinks ruts are added to the traction testing sea of loose rock. After the gully's been negotiated it's over the top and a canter down to Coverdale. A bit of lane then back to track for the last up-hill struggle topped off by a short, sharp drop back to Scar.

SCAR HOUSE RESERVOIR   **1.** Start Scar House Resv car park (GR069766). Turn L (W) for 1.7m (2.7km) – turning R (N) over dam, then L (WNW then W) on track – to T-junction by sheepfolds. **NOTE:** if ground conditions are wet, turn R (N) here and follow

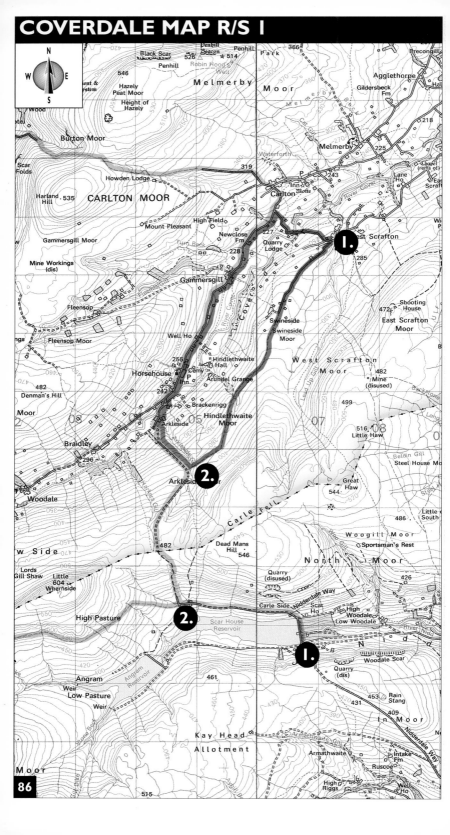

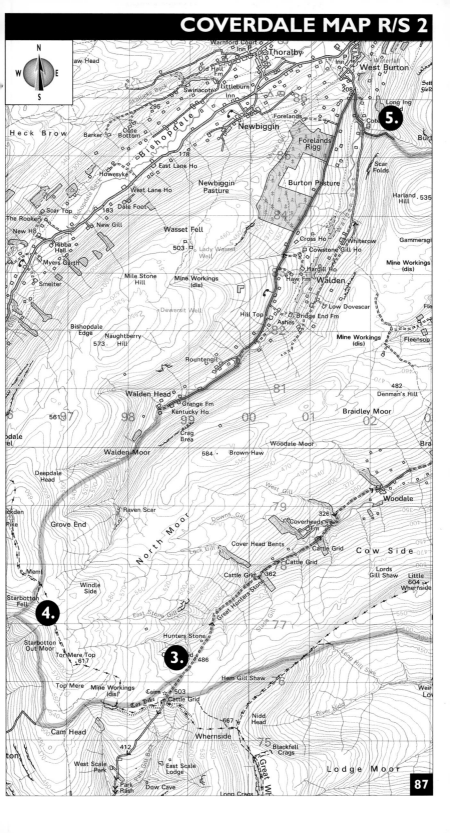

track for 2.5m (4km) to C-road at Arkleside in Coverdale then turn L (SW) for 4.75m (7.6km) to signed T-junction with bridleway. Fork R (SW) and follow directions from para No 3 below.

MAP R/S 2

2. Fork L (SW) for 2.75m (4.4km) – immediately through gap in wall then on boggy grass/peat singletrack, through gate at 0.5m (0.8km), then singletrack roughly contours with marker posts, swinging R (NW) by marker post at 2.4m (3.8km) then turning L (SW) at 2.5m (4km) by wall – to go through gate with waymarker. Keep L (WSW) for 1.6m (2.6km) – by marker post then singletrack dips through very boggy gullies before descending R (NW) at 1.25m (2km) and through gate at 1.5m (2.4km) – to junction with C-road at Coverdale Head. Turn R (NNE) for 0.3m (0.5km) to signed T-junction with bridleway.

COVERDALE HEAD

3. Take hairpin turn L (SW) for 1.75m (2.8km) – track swings R (W) through gate at 0.8m (1.3km), up gully and forking R (WSW, towards Starbotton) at signed bridleway T-junction at 1.5m (2.4km) – to bridleway T-junction immediately after gate. Turn R (N) for 1.4m (2.2km) – through gate at 0.2m (0.3km) then keeping L (N) alongside wall and rejoining track at 0.75m (1.2km) – to bridleway T-junction by cairn on Starbotton Fell.

BUCKDEN PIKE

WALDEN MOOR

4. Turn R (E then NE) for 0.5m (0.8km) – past ruin at 0.25m (0.4km) – to go through gate below Buckden Pike. Keep SO (N) for 1.8m (2.9km) – through spoil heaps, swinging R (NE) at 0.7m (1.15km) (boggy and soft; wheel grabbers!) then steepens at 1.4m (2.2km) (watch out for step on lip!) – to stream confluence below Walden Moor. Cross RH beck. Keep SO (NNE) for 0.8m (1.3km) – on signed singletrack bridleway (not well established) close by Walden Beck, swinging R (E, NE then N) at 0.5m (0.8km) where bridleway squeezes between wall and beck then passing by Kentucky House – to C-road. Turn R (NE) for 4.5m (7.2km) – taking hairpin turn R (S) at 4.0m (6.4km) – to T-junction with bridleway at Cote.

COTE

**MAP
R/S 1**

5. Turn L (SE then E) for 3.0m (4.8km) – swinging R (S then SE) immediately after gate at 0.25m (0.4km), keeping L (SSE, up valley) at T-junction at 0.4m (0.6km), swinging L (E) away from wall at 1.5m (2.4km), zigzagging L/R (effectively SO) (E) through ford at 1.75m (2.8km), watch sharp RH bend at 2.75m (4.4km) and keeping L (ESE) at T-junction soon after – to T-junction with C-road at

CARLTON

Carlton. Turn R (S, towards Horsehouse) for 3.1m (5km) – turning L (S, towards Arkleside) at T-junction with unclassified road at 2.75m (4.4km) – to gated track. Keep SO (SSW then SE) for 2.25m (3.6km) – keeping R (SW) at T-junction at 0.75m (1.2km) and taking care on rough descent starting at 2m (3.2km) – to familiar T-junction by sheepfold. Turn L (E) for 1.7m (2.7km) – following outbound route and taking care on final, rubbly drop to dam – to start.

ROUTE S: COVERDALE (FUN)

MAP R/S 1 (OS 98 & 99)
Distance: 8 miles (13km)
Height-gain: 860ft (260m)
Time: 1.5hrs (dry), 2hrs (wet)
Navigation Skills: easy/moderate
Ride Direction: anti-clockwise

Excellent pot-pourri of lane, track and singletrack with a taste of open fell riding. Ideal for the adventurous tyro.

The climb up from Arkelside's when the work begins but it's soon over. There's a couple of awesome little chasms to cross, the first right after you quit the track. Watch your footing. The next, after a spot of open moor, is rideable if you're experienced.

**WEST
SCRAFTON**

1. Start West Scrafton (GR074836). From telephone box head (SW, towards Carlton) on C-road for 3.6m (5.8km) – turning L (SW, towards Horsehouse and Arkleside) at T-junction at 0.9m (1.4km) and turning L (S, towards Arkleside) at T-junction with unclassified road at 3.3m (5.3km) – to gated track. Keep SO (SSW then SE) for 0.7m

ARKLESIDE

(1.15km) to T-junction with singletrack bridleway immediately after gate.

2. Turn L (NE) for 1m (1.6km) — SO ravine, swinging L (NNE) after gate at 0.5m (0.8km) then following marker posts — to signpost near plantation. Go SO (NE) for 1.25m (2km) — on obvious singletrack bridleway which almost immediately zigzags R/L through ravine, going SO (NE) track X-roads onto singletrack at 0.25m (0.4km) and swinging L (NNE then N) at 0.6m (1km) — to T-junction with bridleway drive at **SWINESIDE**. Go SO (NNE) for 1.1m (1.8km) — going SO (NE) at T-junction with C-road at 1m (1.6km) — to start.

ROUTE T: NIDDERDALE (SPORT)

MAPS T/U 1, T/U 2 (OS 99)
Distance: 22 miles (36km)
Height-gain: 2400ft (730m)
Time: 3hrs (dry), 3.5hrs (wet)
Navigation Skills: easy/moderate
Ride Direction: clockwise

An all-weather circuit complete with tricky drops, testing climbs, a soupçon of singletrack and sea-sized puddles.

Like all good off-road routes the big climbs are on tarmac. Up to Middlesmoor's the first, but before that be prepared for a session of gate-keeping on the farm track from Ramsgill. Middlesmoor marks a welcome return to track; a semi-technical climb quickly followed by a switchback, stone-ridden descent to Scar. Brilliant! It's a flat dash across the dam then a cobbly climb up onto North Moor with views over Nidderdale for company and a radical ravine to up the interest factor. A weaving line along the sides is the only way out of that one! If it's wet mega-puddles make an appearance after Jordan Moss — ideal splash 'n' dash territory — with the ride's technical quotient wrapped up on a sunken track crazily paved with random rubble. Suspension rules! There is a singletrack option for the sensible, stiff-forked brigade — it's on the left.

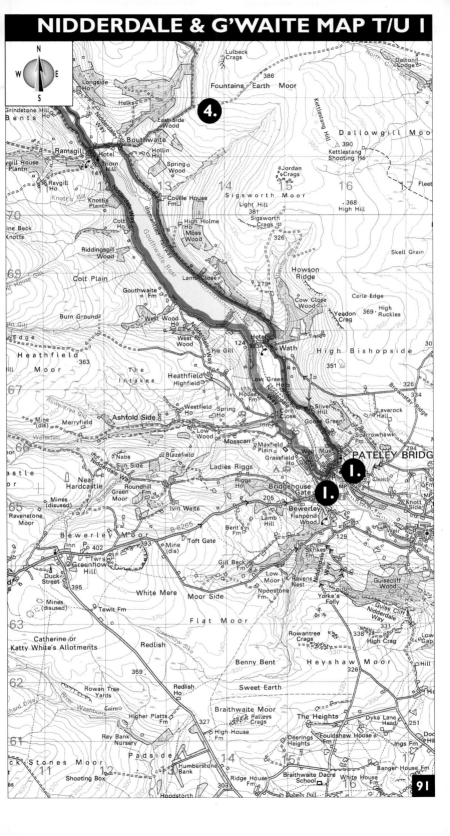

PATELEY BRIDGE

RAMSGILL

MAP T/U 2

1. Start Pateley Bridge long-stay car park (GR158655). Return to X-roads with B6265 in town centre and turn L (SW) for 2.8m (4.5km) – turning R (WNW) just across bridge at 0.2m (0.3km) – to Ramsgill. Fork L (NW) by village green onto gated, farm track for 2.3m (3.7km) – watch out for gate on bend at 1.8m (2.9km) – to T-junction with C-road by bridge.

MIDDLES-MOOR

SCAR HOUSE RESERVOIR

2. Turn R (NE) for 2.8m (4.5km) – over bridge, turning L (WNW, towards Middlesmoor) at T-junction at 0.15m (0.25km), joining track at 1m (1.6km), keeping SO at T-junctions at 1.1m (1.8km) (NW) and at 1.3m (2.1km) (NNW) (gets broken here) and down rough descent at 3.0m (4.8km) – to track T-junction at Scar House Resv. Turn R (E) for 0.6m (1km) – turning L (N) over dam at 0.15m (0.25km) and forking L (WNW) at T-junction at 0.5m (0.8km) – to bridleway T-junction. Turn R (ENE) for 1.1m (1.8km) – going SO track X-roads at 110yds (100m) and over bridge in deep valley at 1m (1.6km) – to track/singletrack bridleway T-junction (easy to miss) in small depression.

3. Fork L (NNW) for 0.5m (0.8km) – on vague singletrack then swinging R (NE then SE) at 0.2m (0.3km) on obvious singletrack – to track T-junction. Keep L (E) for 3.5m (5.6km) – going SO (S) at X-roads at 2m (3.2km) and swinging L (ESE) at 3.1m (5km) – to gated T-junction with C-road. Turn L (NE) for 2.9m (4.6km) – almost immediately turning R (ESE) at T-junction with unclassified road at 110yds (100m), forking R (S) at T-junction at 0.5m (0.8km), keeping R (SSW) at T-junction at 2.3m (3.7km) – to unclassified track T-junction.

MAP T/U 1

BOUTH-WAITE

GOUTH-WAITE RESERVOIR

4. Turn R (SW) for 1m (1.6km) – on gated track with rubbly stretch at 0.7m (1.15km) – to T-junction at Bouthwaite. Turn L (SSE) for 4.6m (7.4km) – alongside Gouthwaite Resv (note spectacular filled quarry at 2.4m/3.8km), turning L (SE) at T-junction at 2.8m (4.5km), keeping SO (towards Pateley Bridge) at all T-junctions – to X-roads with B6265 in Pateley Bridge. Go SO to start.

ROUTE U: GOUTHWAITE (FUN)

MAPS T/U 1, T/U 2 (OS 99)
Distance: 12 miles (20km)
Height-gain: 630ft (190m)
Time: 1hr (dry), 1.5hrs (wet)
Navigation Skills: easy
Ride Direction: either way

Nidderdale escaped being included in the National Park despite being one of the prettiest valleys. This loop's at lake shore level most of the time so don't expect anything exerting.

Ramsgill marks the start of the off-road, it is mainly farm track with nothing more serious than a bit of mud to cope with. Apart from a surprise gate below Blayshaw – speed freaks beware – and a short, sharp cobbled (proper ones) drop that follows soon after. The track alongside Gouthwaite is easy riding but don't forget to take a look at the old quarry just before you get to Wath.

PATELEY BRIDGE

RAMSGILL

MAP T/U 2

1. Start Pateley Bridge long-stay car park (GR158655). Return to X-roads with B6265 in town centre and turn L (SW) for 2.8m (4.5km) – turning R (WNW) at 0.2m (0.3km) just after bridge – to Ramsgill. Fork L (NW) by village green onto gated, farm track for 2.3m (3.7km) – watch out for gate on bend at 1.8m (2.9km) – to T-junction with C-road by bridge.

LOFTHOUSE

MAP T/U 1

2. Turn R (NE) for 2.2m (3.5km) – over bridge, keeping R (NE then SE) at T-junction at 0.15m (0.25km), keeping R (SE, towards Pateley) at T-junction in Lofthouse at 0.4m (0.6km) – to T-junction just before Ramsgill bridge. Turn L (E) for 4.75m (7.6km) – turning R (SSE) at T-junction in Bouthwaite onto track alongside Gouthwaite Resv (note spectacular filled quarry at 2.5m/4km), turning L (SE) at T-junction at 3.0m (4.8km), keeping SO (towards Pateley Bridge) at all T-junctions – to X-roads with B6265 in Pateley Bridge. Go SO to start.

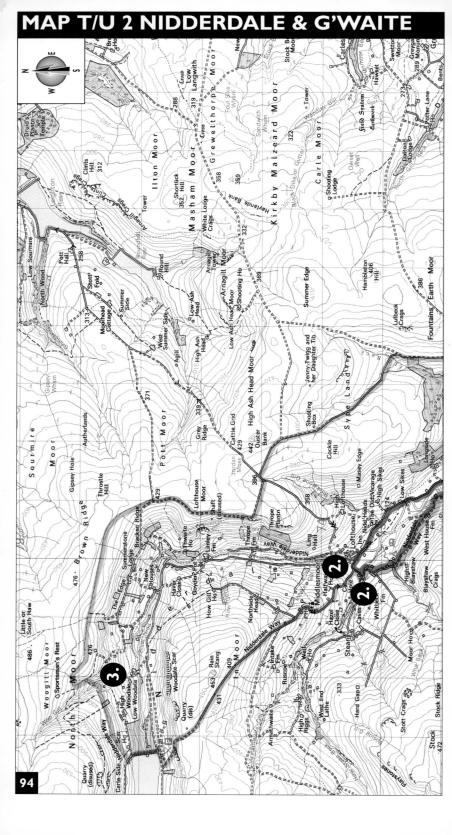

APPENDICES

The following pages are a directory of useful contacts for riders in the Yorkshire Dales, including hostels, bike shops, Forest Enterprise and Tourist Information Centres.

Weather News
☎ 0891 500 418 Yorkshire
☎ 0891 500 419 Cumbria
for Howgill Fells

Tourist Information Centres
Aysgarth Falls
☎ 01969 663424
Hawes
☎ 01969 667450
Kirkby Stephen
☎ 017683 71199
Pateley Bridge
☎ 01423 711147
Sedbergh
☎ 015396 20125
Settle
☎ 01729 825192
Skipton
☎ 01756 792809
YDNP, Grassington
☎ 01756 752748

Youth Hostels
YHA Northern Regional Office
PO Box 11
Matlock
Derbyshire DE4 2XA
☎ 01629 825850

Keld, Swaledale
☎ 01748 886259
Grinton, Swaledale
☎ 01748 884206
Hawes, Wensleydale
☎ 01969 667368

Aysgarth Falls, Wensleydale
☎ 01969 663260
Dentdale, Cowgill
☎ 015396 25251
Ingleton, Lonsdale
☎ 015242 41854
Kettlewell, Wharfedale
☎ 01756 760402
Stainforth, Ribblesdale
☎ 01729 823577
Malham, Craven
☎ 01729 830321
Linton, Wharfedale
☎ 01756 752400

Bunkhouses
Self-catering accommodation in converted barns with full facilities. Ideally suited for mountain bikers:

Barden Tower, Wharfedale (GR051572)
☎ 01756 720616
Dub-Cote, Pen-y-Ghent (GR819715)
☎ 01729 860238
Catholes, Sedbergh (GR653908)
☎ 015396 20334
Halton Gill, Littondale (GR882764)
☎ 01756 770241
Hill Top Farm, Malham (GR899631)
☎ 01729 830320
Grange Farm, Buckden (GR929780)

☎ 01756 760259
Skirfare Bridge Farm, Kilnsey (GR971689)
☎ 01756 752465
The Barnstead, Ingleton (GR686724)
☎ 015242 41386

Further information can be obtained by sending a self-addressed envelope to the YHA Regional Office (address given below).

Other Accommodation
The New Inn,
Appletreewick
Skipton (Wharfedale)
☎ 01756 720252
(The Dales' MTB pub.)

Bike Shops
Northern Dales
Arthur Caygill Cycles
Borough Road
Gallowfields Trading Estate
Richmond
☎ 01748 825469

Southern Dales
Eric Burgess Cycles
Skipton
☎ 01756 794386
JD Bicycle Workshop
Nelson Road
Ilkley
☎ 01943 816101

Chevin Cycles
Leeds Road
Otley
☎ 01943 462773

Western Dales
Settle Cycles
Old Station Yard
Settle
☎ 01729 822216

British Rail Booking Information
☎ 0113 2448133
☎ 01228 44711

Stations are located at:
Skipton, Gargrave, Hellifield, Long Preston, Giggleswick, Preston, Clapham, Bentham and Ilkley.

Yorkshire Dales National Park
Colvend
Hebden Road
Grassington
Skipton
North Yorkshire
BD23 5LB
☎ 01756 752748

Yorkshire County Council
Surveyors Department
County Hall
Northallerton DL7 8AH
☎ 01609 780780

Cumbria County Council
Highways & Transportation
County Offices
Kendal
Cumbria LA9 4RG

Forest Enterprise (NE England)
1a Grosvenor Terrace
York YO3 7BD
☎ 01434 220242

The Cyclist's Touring Club
Since 1878 the Cyclist's Touring Club (CTC) has been the governing body for recreational cycling in this country and is recognised by such organisations as the Sports Council, the Department of Transport and the Department of the Environment. Membership is open to anyone interested in cycling. They currently have 40,000 members, 200 nation-wide clubs and 100 local clubs affiliated to them.

Recently the CTC has taken on responsibility for addressing off-road cycling access issues which includes promoting Rights of Way initiatives

wherever they occur and representing the views of mountain bikers at a local and national levels. Local representation is done through a network of volunteer Access Officers.

If you would like to apply for membership then please apply to:
CTC
Dept CSB/94
69 Meadrow
Godalming
Surrey GU7 3HS
☎ 01483 417217.

Benefits of being a member include: Representation on Rights of Way and access issues in your area; third-party insurance cover; free legal advice for cycling related problems; free legal aid; free technical advice; free international touring information; bi-monthly colour magazine; free handbook; mail order service; a voice in the world of MTBing.